IT'S MICK NOT MIKE

IT'S MICK NOT MIKE

THE AUTOBIOGRAPHY OF MICK DUXBURY

BY MICK DUXBURY WITH WAYNE BARTON

First published by Pitch Publishing, 2015

Pitch Publishing
A2 Yeoman Gate
Yeoman Way
Durrington
BN13 3QZ
www.pitchpublishing.co.uk

A CIP catalogue record is available for this book
from the British Library.

ISBN 978-1-78531-049-2

Typesetting and origination by Pitch Publishing

Printed by TJ International, Cornwall, UK

Contents

To Karen, wife and best friend

Acknowledgements

To Wayne, for the belief, time and effort in bringing this book to fruition. Thanks to Paul and Jane at Pitch Publishing for getting it down in to print!

Foreword by Bryan Robson

WHEN I joined Manchester United, Mick was typical of what I expected to find. Hard-working, conscientious, and dedicated to his profession. And professional is the key word for him because you knew you would get that from him in every single match he played. His discipline was good too – he'd always be one of the first in for training and would carry out the instructions from the manager on to the pitch when it came to matchday.

Sometimes you would get players who came into training and just wanted to muck about but Mick was serious; he trained like he played, and that for me was part of what made him such a good player.

He had already developed that kind of reputation in the game and when I saw it first hand I was able to confirm it for myself. There was no room for slackness with him and it set the standard, not just for the new players like myself, but for younger lads who would watch us train and play.

He was a really good lad, too. He was quiet and kept himself to himself – on the pitch, he was an organiser, but he wasn't a shouter who would bollock a team-mate. He'd leave that to the gobshites like me! But we complemented each other well and in fact often played together in midfield. That versatility was part of why Ron Atkinson really liked him. He was a great right-back but he would do a good job for you in midfield or wherever he played.

Mick and I enjoyed some successes together at Old Trafford, mostly in the FA Cup. It was a team of blends, where everyone brought something different, and Mick's hard-working ethic and professionalism were instrumental. That was Mick – seven or eight out of ten every week. He'd never let you down and his skill set was undoubtedly part of the reason we were a good team.

At a club like United you'll always have fierce competition. Ron was trying to build a squad and I can understand that once players come in who play in your position that you can feel threatened or as if the manager doesn't fancy you. That's football. I still speak to Ron and he talks very highly of Mick's professionalism and quality as a player, and it's a testament to his ability that he outlasted all of the players brought in and fought off some competition from good players.

As I mentioned, Mick's versatility was a good trait, and that, coupled with his attitude, made him a valuable player for managers to have around. First, Dave Sexton, who brought him in, and then Ron, and then Alex Ferguson. That reminds me of a story – we were coming back from an away game on the coach and the gaffer and I were looking for people to make up the numbers in our card school. Mick, who normally never played, joined in with us. As we're playing we're giving each other a general knowledge football quiz and we got around to asking the gaffer to name all of the players to have played for England with the letter 'x' in their surname. I think there were seven at the time, and the gaffer got six, but hadn't yet named Mick. Mick was sat next to the boss and is almost pulling behind so as not to make it obvious – we're all killing ourselves laughing. After a while he gets it and throws the cards down in a strop!

Maybe that story sums Mick up – he went about his business so well and without any fuss. Managers keep players like Mick because they are so valuable and that's why he remained at Old Trafford as long as he did.

I think he certainly had the ability and athleticism to have remained at United a little while longer, to have been part of the squad that won the European Cup Winners' Cup or even the league trophy he wanted so badly. I can sympathise because I was fortunate enough to just benefit from some of that avalanche of success United enjoyed. He was unlucky in both respects, not just missing out on the league, but also in Europe as he (like the rest of us) didn't get the opportunity to play in Europe after our 1985 win. Of course it is always sad to see someone who you have shared a dressing room with and always respected move on.

He was such a good player that he was rewarded with international caps and we played a few times for club and country, including the famous win we enjoyed together for England in the Maracana. Our last professional encounter came as I was coaching for the national side and Mick played for a select side against us just before Euro 1996. That was his retirement game, and we had a good few pints together afterwards.

We haven't seen much of each other since but that doesn't surprise me – he always kept himself to himself. That's not to say he didn't join in with us when we were out on tour but he would leave the mischief to McGrath, Whiteside and myself. But that was Mick, and his professionalism. He gave a good, honest 100 per cent every time, the perfect type of player for a manager. He perhaps had a lot more ability than people maybe give him credit for – it's an obvious point for me, not least because he played almost 400 times for Manchester United, but also because he had the footballing intelligence to perform in a number of positions and perform to a high standard – and I'm proud to have called him a team-mate for so long.

1

Natural Progression

NATURAL progression. It's a phrase that I thought and talked a lot about when deciding to write my story and when I actually started putting it in to words. It summarises much of my early development and movement into the sport with which I would become most recognised.

I was always for the outdoors; you could always find me playing out, whether it was playing football, other sports, or just as kids mucking around. We lived on a terraced street with a close neighbourhood and any free time would be spent going out with my mates. Not that I wanted to be away from my family. I suppose I had your normal upbringing, there was a lot of love and affection in the family, but I was always one to be playing outside, especially in the summer holidays. First thing, it'd be 'what are you doing today?' and the answer was 'going out!' You'd call on someone and get three or four of you in a group. We'd go all around but there was one place we'd gravitate to more often than others and that was 'the Square'. Its posh name was 'Nelson Square', but it was only a piece of waste ground, so I don't know why it had a posh name as such! It was surrounded by fencing but there was just enough of a gap to squeeze between or slide underneath it to get in.

There, we'd just have a game of footy, play cowboys and indians, cops and robbers or other games that had less politically correct titles which seemed harmless when you were kids but not the kind of things you'd want to repeat in this day and age. We'd go scrambling on our bikes, go down the river to try and catch some sticklebacks, climbing trees… really, just the typical things you would expect of any normal boy, the kind of things you would hope that one can experience.

Dad worked down the pit at Huncoat Colliery which sadly closed down in 1968 in the Bevan Closures. Mum had a few jobs but the one I remember most was when she worked at a local factory called Rist Wires which had a predominantly female workforce; of a morning, dad would be up and out early, mum would get me and my older sister, Anne, ready for school and then get ready for work herself. Six years after me, our younger sister Louise came along, too. We were able to just walk around to our local junior school which was only three or four streets away. It was Sacred Heart Primary, situated in an old Victorian building which has since been knocked down and replaced by a newer school adjacent to it.

We had a good childhood, there was always food on the table and clothes on our backs. We managed to go away on day trips to the coast on a Sunday, or down the Ribble Valley where we'd take a picnic. I think, as much as anything, it was good for mum and dad to get out and do something and forget about work for a few hours, but we certainly appreciated the value of how hard they worked.

I grew up in Accrington on Russia Street – my mum and dad still live in the same house today. We lived halfway down the street and Philip Riley lived half a dozen doors down from us; Philip was about a week older than me. His nickname was Dylan after the rabbit in the children's TV programme Magic Roundabout. Down the street from us both was Steven

Preston… his nickname was Fred, though I can't tell you why that was the case! Mine was Dux, for obvious reasons, although I'm sure I was called worse.

That was the core of our group, though there were a few more who would hang around with us. I didn't have an older brother but Philip did, called Steven, and Steven had one called Martin. There would always be someone to knock around with in a group… we'd get into scrapes, nothing crazy or in any trouble that would get the police involved. Sometimes there'd be fights with other gangs of lads, that sort of thing, but it wasn't ever anything serious. Not like it could have been anyway, as we never travelled too far – everything was centred around your two or three streets or on to the Square. We had a fairly big family – I had a cousin, Tony, who had emigrated to Canada but came back at the age of seven or eight. I'd go up on my bike to see them on a Sunday morning, and we'd go and see my grandma and granddad on my dad's side quite regularly as they only lived three or four streets away. We had a bit of a scam going on – if there was an ice cream van, we'd get money from grandma to get one, and then leg it around to our house and do the same to mum and dad as well! I don't think they cottoned on – sorry!

One day we went up to the Square and there was a post with a notice on, informing us that as from such and such a date, there would be work starting on building a new sports centre on the wasteland. I think 99 per cent of the community rejoiced, but us as kids were gutted that our play area was being taken away! Work commenced, and I was in secondary school by this stage; I went to school in Blackburn, and Steven went to school in Accrington, so I didn't see too much of the group I grew up with when we were kids. In fact, it could well have been around the time that I joined United.

As construction began on the Square there were lots of earth-moving machines, diggers, JCBs and the like. I don't think there was the same kind of security as you would find nowadays; one evening, Steven went up there by himself (I think), got into the site and climbed into one of the diggers. It turned over on him and tragically killed him – I was a couple of years older than him, so he must have only been 13 or 14 at the time. He was such a lovely lad – never the brightest, but he'd do anything for you and was always laughing and joking and being a bit mischievous. Maybe mischievous is the wrong word, as he was just being a normal lad. The story goes further, however.

The Hyndburn Sports Centre was opened by David Lloyd in 1976 and since then, my wife Karen has worked there in a part-time job – in fact, that's where I met her – and our two sons worked there as leisure assistants. We've always, then, had such a connection with the place, and although Karen and I knew about the history, the boys never did.

One night, Ashley, our eldest son, came home and we were sat having a chat around the table and the conversation, as it does, got to work. Ashley was telling us that he'd seen 'the ghost' again. We asked what he was on about, so he said that there was talk of a ghost there and it was well known that it would pop up every now and again. There was a cafe up above the swimming pool, sort of like a viewing area, and Ashley said that the last people in the centre when it was empty would see a young lad up there. Or, when they'd go to the table tennis area and clear the tables away, turn the lights off and lock the door, the lights would come back on. It was a regular occurrence and there'd often be sightings. As you would, I felt it was strange and asked Ashley if he'd ever seen the ghost, and he hadn't, though he'd been in places in the centre and it'd not felt right. At the same time, Karen and I looked at each other, both with the same question in the back of our minds. 'Have you given the ghost a name?' I asked. The reply came, 'Fred'! The hairs on my neck still go up thinking about it!

So, apparently, the ghost is meant to be that of Steven… there are sightings of him in the sauna area, too, which is the site of where the digger was when he attempted to climb in it. I have to be honest and say that I haven't seen it, or been up there at a time when I might have. I'm not sure I'd want to!

To pick up some pocket money I'd help our local milkman, Tony. He would come around on his milk float and we just got to know him over the years. I'd jump on outside the house and then help him with one or two bottles down the road, and run back up… eventually, I was allowed to do a few streets. It went from that to six streets, then half the round, then I'd do the full round. I'd go up to Tony and Margaret's (his partner) for breakfast and then do the milk round. At times I was able to do it and fit it around school. Thinking about it now, the athletic nature of jumping up and down on the float, the sprinting to put the bottles down, all helped to prepare me for my sporting lifestyle. Dylan joined in too, so it became competitive.

I remember once, Tony was yelling at us to get going. He started the float and I jumped on, Dylan jumped on but could only grab on by his hands. I cringe when I think about recounting this story based on what is accepted these days but there was Dylan, being dragged along and holding on… he climbed on and we laughed and joked about it. It's unbelievable to think about what might have happened.

The friendship between ours and Tony's family continued to last; we chose Tony to be godfather to the kids and Margaret is godmother to one of them. Sadly Tony died a few years ago in his mid-60s from a rare form of motor neurone disease that affects something like one in a million; Marg still lives round the corner from us and we see her often and their children Joanne and Michael. Margaret and Tony were part of my testimonial committee, too. It might be that when I retire I'll take up the milk round again – funnily enough, after I went to

Hong Kong in the 1990s and came back to England looking for something to do, I did the milk round for a month!

I did it from 5am to 8am, and then when I managed to get a job teaching, for the first week I did my notice – I continued to do the round and then went straight to school. I was Ernie, the fastest milk cart in the west!

Dad was into his sports so it was always going to be the case that I was too. He loved it – he loved his football, from either playing for the colliery teams, or going to watch Burnley play in the old First Division. He was also a boxer, only on a local basis, but it was something he really loved. I grew to love it too, and we'd sometimes spar just for fun at home. I'd never go to see him fight, though. It was just something he did, I can't remember him coming back with any cuts or bruises.

The one injury I do remember him picking up was through a work accident; one of the areas he was working in collapsed and he got some shrapnel in his eye. There was a knock on the door and mum answered to the news dad was in hospital. He was in there for a long time with a patch over his eye and we went as often as we could despite mum not driving. He was okay after that, thankfully, but his eye was never the same though he wasn't blinded. I don't think he boxed after that. Mum was into her sports, too, she played netball, but when we kids came along, she didn't have the same time for it.

In a female-dominated household it has to be said that Saturday afternoons with my dad were special – even with more girls than boys, I think they often got a bit annoyed with us as we would do what dad wanted to do most of the time. We'd spend much of the time together, though, taking in as much football as possible. Burnley on a Saturday afternoon, but also the youth team games and reserve games as well. I can remember being there for a midweek game when Manchester United came to Turf Moor, I think it must have been around 1970 as I'm sure it was the first year I was in secondary school. Their fans took over the entire ground, and I think United won 1-0.

As well as supporting Burnley I know dad really enjoyed it when he got to see the best teams and the top players and at the time there was no reason to think Burnley couldn't have been part of that. They were dubbed 'The Team of the Seventies' at the time although it never really turned out that way. They had players like Ralph Coates and Martin Dobson, good players, and Burnley got as far as the FA Cup semi-final in 1974 when they played against Newcastle, but sadly they were beaten by a brace of goals from Malcolm Macdonald. I remember going to Hillsborough to be there for that great occasion; it was enjoyable watching them, and though they'd never quite reach the potential they were tipped for or the greatness they'd experienced when I was just an infant and they won the league in 1960, it was always entertaining at Turf Moor.

It seems funny to suggest it now but at the time it was Burnley or Blackburn as your local team, and Blackburn were struggling, so Burnley were the more attractive choice. It helped that they had glamorous European nights welcoming the likes of Napoli, especially in those early days of continental competition. I know I did go to some of them, but it was at an age where I was too young to recall any memories to share, sadly.

Likewise, I was too young to remember the 1960 Burnley team but just old enough to remember the World Cup Final in 1966. FA Cup Final day was always a day where the women would leave the house to do the shopping and dad and I would sit in all day and watch the game and the build-up on television, but on the day of the World Cup Final, we all sat inside to watch England play Germany. It is such a vivid memory; nowadays I don't scream and shout at the television when I'm watching a game but certainly on that particular day I did, especially when Germany scored late on to send it into extra time. 'Offside ref!' – you're just claiming anything, aren't you! The celebrations afterwards, when Geoff Hurst scored that hat-trick goal to secure the greatest moment in English football history, were memorable. I was Geoff, on the cobbled streets outside afterwards. There was a schoolhouse across the road and it had been built on a slope so there was just enough of a wall to make a goal from. A natural goal for us to go outside and play football with, if there were ten minutes to spare to have a quick kickabout before our tea was ready.

That was the case with much of my early life, every spare minute spent doing something active. When you're young, you go out and play around in your gangs, and then as you get a bit older you do something a bit more productive and organised. I was always running, climbing and jumping around; if there was a tree to be climbed or something to be collected from up high I was always the one to be doing it. Around this time I passed my 11 plus which gave me the opportunity to go to St Mary's College in Blackburn. It was a school with a wonderful reputation both on and off the sports field. There were plenty of opportunities to participate in as many sports as I could, with the guidance of the PE teacher Mr Duckworth who was really into his sports, be it swimming, athletics or football. I'd always played football, even in primary school, and managed to be selected for the Accrington town team which was really good. I can still remember some of my team-mates from that time and I do see them around town still.

At St Mary's, I recall we had the traditional sports days at the end of the year which were held in Witton Park in Blackburn which is a well-known local place for hosting sports. I was into my hurdling, long jump, cross country… well, I wasn't overly keen on cross country running, but it was something that I was naturally good at. Through winning school events, I was asked to represent Blackburn at cross country – the one thing I never did quite get the hang of was playing cricket. I played it, but never at a level that would be considered competitive. I'm not quite sure I ever got the hang of the technique required. My parents were happy for me to do whatever I wanted on that side of things (as long as it was within reason) and being so young I never really considered that there was any pressure on me, even when representing the town.

I was always nervous. At school, you always knew who you were playing with or competing against but when you're up for your town it's a whole new group of children you don't know; in a way, I think that may have helped me and stood me in good stead for later on. It wasn't a hindrance for me; and meeting new people, particularly for the first few times, isn't always easy for me, so having had the experience to get used to it from an early age was something that can only have helped. The discipline itself – the physical and mental preparation for the event – was second nature to me, it was the social integration I would always find harder.

Yet pressure was something that wasn't applied to me, or it certainly wasn't something I personally felt. You would hear stories through the grapevine about local players or athletes that you would find yourself up against, 'he's been at such and such a club', but dad would always say to me that reputations count for nothing. 'Kick him and he'll scream, cut him and he'll bleed,' those kind of things to put it across that you weren't up against anything supernatural, and it helped prepare me and take it in my stride. It might be true to suggest that to other players and teams, those kind of things were being said about me, but that wasn't something I thought about or realised at the time.

Over recent years one or two people have come up to me if I've been having a drink or out in the street and they've said, 'I thought I was a good player but then I came up against you and I'd heard all about you, they were right, I couldn't get near you, you were quicker, faster, had more skill.' It's a funny coincidence that since I've decided to write my story, I've noticed more people saying nice things. I was playing a game with the United legends team in Belfast and their manager, a lad called David Jeffrey, he's been there for about 17 years and done really well. I'm doing him a disservice – he's been the most successful manager in Linfield's history, winning 31 trophies in 17 years! That was after playing for them for ten seasons as well. He was actually an apprentice at United (I think he was from the years between Andy Ritchie coming through and Mark Hughes and Clayton Blackmore) and I hadn't seen him for years. After exchanging niceties, he said that as apprentices they were all striving to be like me, that I was always doing things right and professionally. Honestly, I'd never thought like that – it's nice to hear, but until recently, it was always me thinking that way about other people.

Whether I was talented or not is something that's for other people to judge and assess but I can certainly confirm my dedication. There are things that you learn and pick up from your footballing education but there are also personal qualities in each and every individual – something must be in there to start with.

We're all different but my upbringing is something that I feel can only have been beneficial and conducive to the career I was going to have. There was never any pressure, only encouragement, all positive things. Even when negative things happened. I didn't manage to get into England schoolboys as a kid but it was like, 'That was unlucky, but it happens, just wait for the next opportunity.' There's something in you when you're born but it has to be nurtured in the right way – and thankfully, I was raised in an environment that helped.

Much of it, of course, is down to that natural progression. At the end of primary school I had managed to get into the Accrington under-11 town team so if things were to progress at their natural speed, I would be looking to go on to play football for my secondary school. It might surprise some who followed my career but I started off as a striker; I don't know if that's just something that the teachers did, choosing your better players to go up front… it certainly can't be said that we had a poor team, as we had a good team with good players throughout. It was a good school for football, there were one or two lads in there that went on to play professionally as well as me.

In the first year we played Bacup and Rawtenstall Grammar School up on a horrible pitch over in Rossendale. It was right on top of the Moors, if you kicked the ball over the edge it went for miles. We won something like 12-1 and I scored five. We were beating good teams, coming up against Manchester Grammar School, and ended up getting to the Schools Cup Final where we played at Ewood Park against Billinge School. It was so exciting in the build-up as you can imagine, a group of kids getting to play on a professional ground, but as we came out of the dressing room and on to the pitch we discovered that they'd made the pitch a lot smaller – as you'd expect they would do – and that disappointed us all, with us striving to try and score in the big professional goals. We won anyway.

They had a lad called Paul Biggins who was one of those who came with a big reputation, but funnily enough I scored a hat-trick in the 4-1 result. Mr Duckworth did a report for the school bulletins and I can remember him writing, 'Duxbury, harassed as he was by two defenders, managed to shrug them off and slide it past the keeper into the back of the net.' Funny how praise stays with you isn't it… in my opinion that's much better than being negative. They were good times, and the side that we had stayed together more or less throughout our secondary school years, enjoying much success along the way.

There was an emphasis on sport at the school and at the end of the term, we'd be taken camping up to Ennerdale in our team. It wasn't like a pre-season but just a get-away in a semi-detached bungalow near a youth hostel up in the Lake District. We'd walk through the days in the fells and play football in the evenings; there was the Ennerdale agricultural show which included traditional lakeland sports such as fell racing and trail hounds, sports which are still thriving to this day. We were all enthusiastic to begin with but it was the hardest thing I'd ever done! There were six rosettes to be awarded; you'd run along the lake, and then up and down the fell. You're falling and sliding all over the place; it was difficult, but I managed to come sixth and be the only one from our team with a rosette. Mum's still got it to this day, but like I say, it was the most difficult physical thing I've ever been through in my life!

We were 12 and 13, and we had a sixth-former looking after us. The teachers would go to a pub which was about three miles away and we'd be left in this cottage with a 19-year-old and an open fire and old gas lights; there was no fridge, so we had to get milk from outside. Nobody wanted to go and get the milk, everyone was too scared! It's unbelievable; it was superb at the time but I look at it now as a teacher and think it was a disaster waiting to happen. It's funny, though, but we weren't into looking for trouble. Our idea of fun was standing books on a table to make a makeshift table tennis net and play over that, or spend money at the tuck shop which the sixth-former would be looking after. The most risky thing we did was going down to swim in the river, which even in August or September would be absolutely freezing. We do outdoor pursuits at the school where I'm now working but with the limitations and boundaries which you would expect in the modern age; you can't help but feel some of the magic has been lost but maybe that's as much to do with nostalgia as I can certainly appreciate how dangerous it could have been!

Incidentally, talking about that Schools Cup Final match, I can also remember my very first game for the primary school team. We didn't have a pitch so we'd get taken in a minibus to play on King George's playing fields, where I had often watched my dad play. There were only a couple of pitches that were level, right by the changing rooms. The school pitch was one of the furthest away from the changing rooms, though, and the slope was quite severe – you had to be mountain goats to play on it, with one leg shorter than the other! I remember playing in red shirts with laces in and black shorts – there was a playground at the side, with railings, and we'd be expected to change there and hang our clothes on the railings. After the game, I couldn't find my trousers (I'd been wearing long shorts), and thought, 'Somebody's nicked 'em.' I was panicking, thinking that when I'd get home my mum would give me what for. It wasn't until I'd been there for a while that I realised that the shorts I was wearing were that big and baggy that I'd put them on over my school shorts! I looked like Billy Casper from *Kes* – I remember the shorts incident more than the game itself!

It was through playing for the school that I began to get attention from professional clubs; there weren't academies, or the same kind of youth set-up as it is these days. You'd either get picked up from playing trials held for local boys at the clubs or from being watched or noticed by a scout when you were playing for the school. We had some teachers involved at some of the local clubs as well, which helped some players get picked up, and you would always sort of know when scouts were coming and which club they'd be from. Personally, I never let myself think that they were coming to watch me and I think that was for the best; knowing me, having that on my mind would affect my performance.

Regardless of my own desire to shut it out, it happened anyway, and scouts would approach dad and talk about me, asking if it'd be possible if I could go for trials. That sort of attention began to come when I was 12 or 13 and when it came to holidays, I'd go and spend a couple of days at different clubs. Burnley was one I was naturally holding out for, being my club. They also had a great reputation for developing young players and giving them a chance but the funny thing is that I never even went for a trial there. I don't even think they asked – I'm sure if dad had been asked, then I would have gone there. I went to Blackburn a few times, Rochdale a couple of times… I think the Rochdale trial came about as the scout was the dad of one of my schoolmates. Everton and Liverpool made enquiries – it was mainly the north-west clubs, though I was asked to go down to Arsenal and Norwich, too. It was just too far.

I did go down to Leeds – probably more often than any other club – they had a local club called Pudsey Juniors, a club that Leeds would pick their youth players from, and a club that I represented on a few occasions. We actually went on tour with them to Lille in northern France and with the experiences I was having there, it might have been expected that I would eventually end up at Elland Road. Leeds and Liverpool were fantastic clubs and still are, big clubs with a proud history, yet at the time I was still disappointed that Burnley hadn't yet come in for me!

Manchester United didn't really come in to the picture right until the end, funnily enough. In fact, had fate twisted a different way, I might well have ended up at one of their most hated opponents. I went to Everton for a trial and I have to say that their training facilities were beautiful, they really turned my head, but it was their cross-city rivals that made a really serious move for me.

Myself and a lad from school named Peter Betts, a big, strong lad, were invited up to Liverpool to watch a game and offered us schoolboy terms. We both signed them at Anfield, but in order to complete the agreement, we needed our school headmaster to sign off on it. The day after, we came away and thought about it and I felt a little bit uneasy about it. The reality of moving to Liverpool and staying in digs was something I was contemplating and it wasn't a prospect I was really looking forward to (no disrespect intended to the city!). I had a few sleepless nights and I ended up speaking to Peter – it came to light that he felt the same as me, and so, encouraged by the confidence in unity, we told our parents and the headmaster that we didn't want him to sign the forms. My dad rung Liverpool to inform them of my change of heart. You never know how things might have turned out!

A little while afterwards, United came in for me and made an offer. It was something I immediately felt a lot more comfortable with in myself so I was more than happy to sign schoolboy terms with them. There was still never a word of persuasion either way from my parents, who left it up to me. They might have been quite happy for me to sign for Liverpool, but by the time it came to signing for United, I think they just wanted me to sign for someone, anyone! As long as I was safe, they were happy. It was a choice entirely made by myself and I was delighted and confident that I'd made the right one. Football can be funny in the way that paths take different people; I never regretted my choice but perhaps Peter did. It was through my own disappointment at missing out with England Schoolboys that I was noticed by United in the first place, with their scouts Gordon Clayton and Norman Scholes watching on. The trials were up at Scunthorpe; there was only myself who went up from Blackburn and I travelled up with one of the teachers, who wasn't even a teacher of mine. I don't think that would be allowed to happen nowadays! Early on the Saturday morning he picked me up at the top of our street and we went up there. I didn't play particularly well, I didn't think, so I wasn't surprised that I wasn't selected if they were just going from that particular game.

If I remember correctly, Norman and Gordon came around to our house afterwards. They must have done as we weren't on the phone to get in touch with us that way. I was banished out of the room as it was a formal meeting; kind of like when you go to a parents' meeting at school. At the end of the meeting, I was brought in and invited to the club and it went from there.

I insist that I still didn't necessarily feel any pressure. With no disrespect to the likes of Bolton or Leeds, Liverpool and Manchester United were two of the biggest clubs in the world. If I had any anxiety at all it was more to do with how I would settle into things away from football rather than on the pitch. If you could just transport me into my kit and boots and put me on the field with a ball, that would be the easy bit. Sitting in a changing room with people I didn't know, getting on a minibus with them to get to a game, that was going to be the hard part for me. United did their best to encourage social interaction, taking us for a group meal at the Cafe Royal in Manchester. That kind of thing did impress me and did help, and I moved into digs during the summer of 1976 which also encouraged me to maybe come out of my shell a little more.

Moving in to digs was a decision I did deliberate over; I eventually decided to do so, with the comfort and knowledge that I was not so far away from home. If anything went wrong, I knew I was only a bus ride from home. My digs were at 45 Lostock Road in Davyhulme near David Herd's garage, with Mrs Williams. United had just had a recruitment of new landladies and she was part of them, so myself and a Welsh lad called David Haggart were her first lodgers. Dave was a year younger than me but was brought up on a permanent basis from Pontypridd to go to school locally as he was that highly thought of. We shared digs for the first year – Mrs Williams was a lovely lady, and David and I weren't too much of a problem for her. I'd go home quite often, catching a bus for the 45-minute journey home.

For Dave it wasn't quite that easy. There's the story at the club of Brian Greenhoff and Sammy McIlroy, and Sammy found it difficult but Brian helped him settle. I don't think I was quite as helpful as Brian was and maybe that didn't help David. Having said that, I'm not sure that it would have helped him coming back to my home, or whether that would have made it worse. We had some other Welsh lads at the club so David would mingle with them at the weekends; the club paid for them to go home once every month if they wanted to, otherwise they were expected to stay. I don't know if that was selfish on my part or whether anything I did would have really helped.

I did stay the odd time, and go out with some of the others. At first we obviously didn't know many of the kids at the club and we didn't like lounging around Mrs Williams's home so we'd get out as much as we could. Dad would keep in touch by going up to the phone box and ringing Mrs Williams's house but we would often be up the phone box ourselves for David to ring his parents or me to ring my friends. It would be a while until I met Karen, but I was still in those digs when we started seeing each other.

At night we'd go to the cinema, Stretford Sports Centre or the Garricks Head which was a nice pub near Davyhulme Golf Club. We'd never drink, it would be a blackcurrant and lemonade and a game of Space Invaders on the arcade machines. We spent a lot of time together but the worst time for David would be that time after the game on Saturday; we'd play our match, then go to Old Trafford to watch the first team, and my dad would come to the game to watch me and then watch

United with me. I'd go home with him and Dave would be left at Mrs Williams's by himself.

The house was a lovely detached house, we had plenty of room, and we'd get our breakfast and dinner which were always delicious. It was only a bus ride from Old Trafford, where Norman Davies would pick us up and drive us to The Cliff. Whereas David might have felt a substantial change in his life, for me, it was very much as I said at the start – natural progression. All I wanted to do was play the game and I was eager to get a chance to play for the biggest club in the country.

2

Hard Work Beats Talent When Talent Doesn't Work Hard

I SAID that Manchester United were the biggest club in Britain and I stand by that. When I joined the club as a schoolboy in the summer of 1976 they had just enjoyed their first season back in the First Division after a turbulent few years and the feeling around the club was very much one of regeneration. The style of play under Tommy Docherty was flamboyant and the mood around Old Trafford was buoyant; the club had finished third and reached the FA Cup Final. I was still at school at the time, of course, but I went to the game prior to arriving at the club in July as an apprentice.

I can remember my dad being so excited to go down. I was too – we'd never been to an FA Cup Final. We got up at a ridiculous hour, maybe 4am or 5am, and travelled down to London in a Morris 1100 where we arrived easily before 9am. We spent the next four hours just wandering around, but how many times can you do that? The atmosphere was great to soak up when the fans started arriving but I must confess that I was a little bit disappointed with Wembley Stadium. We had a walk all around, round the back to the areas that you wouldn't see on pictures or the television. When you came down to Wembley Way and the twin towers everything looked magnificent but when you go around the back, everything just looked a little bit shabby, and I'm sad to say that I felt terribly underwhelmed. That was something that stayed with me for a while, and I suppose that wasn't helped by the result on the day.

There was excitement during the game – you're part of it, in a way, shouting and screaming, and you get involved, though of course I didn't feel the same disappointment as the players on the day. I didn't have the same emotional connection at that point, but that wasn't down to my Burnley background.

I might have been a little bit happier two years later but that's not to say that I ever hated United, I'd grown up with that respect and even a jealousy that I can admit to. I grew up with banter with the United fans in school but I was never going to be shouting for Southampton in the final; in a way, it was that game and the Liverpool one I'd attended which sort of started my love affair with the club. Despite my relatively poor impression of Wembley, one thing that did stay with me in a positive way was the incredible atmosphere. I'd go on to play for United at Wembley on a number of occasions and after playing in front of 50,000 at Old Trafford you learn to control the noise but you can certainly notice it as a supporter when there are 100,000 fans at Wembley going crazy. It's an intense experience. Crowds of 12,000 or 13,000 at Burnley were good and could create noise but as I already mentioned, it was a different story when United came to town.

That United team who just lost out in 1976 had the likes of Jimmy Nicholl, Brian Greenhoff and Sammy McIlroy, players who had come through the system, and you knew that if you joined United then you had a good chance of either making it or at least getting the chance to do so. Liverpool, on the other hand, tended to work the other way – they'd buy players in, give them half a season of preparation in the reserves to test them out and then try them in the first team. United did still buy some players in, every club does, but it was about getting the balance right and the message under Tommy seemed to be that if you were good enough you'd get your chance.

Because you're part of it and you've grown up with it, it's difficult to explain or articulate the allure of United. I remember there was a game I attended when I was a schoolboy, it was against Liverpool one midweek under the floodlights. I was sat there thinking, 'Wow, this is unbelievable.' It was a game of football but it was on a different level to anything that I'd ever known. It was a special feeling, but one that is hard to put into words. The atmosphere, as I've said, was incredible. I'd always heard of people saying about the special buzz you get at Old Trafford for an evening game in midweek but experiencing it was a very, very exciting thing.

This was at a time when hooligan culture was rife yet there was no feeling of intimidation. Things went on, of course, but I was lucky in that I didn't really feel anything like that. It wasn't just one pocket, it was an atmosphere that filled the ground and when you're a kid who's just signed terms at the club there is nothing that can motivate you more than witnessing something like that and thinking that if you try your best then one day you can be playing in front of it. Everything, all the hairs on your body would tingle and it would definitely whet the appetite.

Maybe the best way that I can describe it is by comparison; years later we had travelled to an away game and Liverpool were playing away too, the day before, so we went along to watch. I can't remember where it was but I think it was somewhere like Luton. The atmosphere wasn't the same at all. Liverpool took supporters but it wasn't the same as our travelling fans; the home fans, too, weren't the same. There wasn't the same kind of electricity in the air, the same tension and the ground wasn't full. The one thing that stayed in my mind was how lucky we were to play in front of what we did every single week home or away. Other clubs didn't get it but it brought it home to us, and certainly me, and it made me appreciate it a lot more.

There was a difference standing on the terraces at Turf Moor as a supporter and being among the Manchester United supporters as a young player for the club. At the time I didn't sit down and analyse it and looking back and appreciating it maybe that too was for the best. These big events were happening to me, signing for United, watching them play and being part of it, but I was taking it all in my stride. Had I stopped and thought about it, maybe it might have got to me a little bit more. There was obviously a different internal feeling; as a supporter, you're stood willing your team on and hoping for the best. As a young player, when you're surrounded by these walls of noise, it motivates you to want to go and produce and get the chance to play in front of such passion. Like I've explained, playing was almost like the easy part of it all for me.

Thankfully I didn't have the same troubles of settling that David Haggart had but I was still not exactly at my most comfortable when socialising with the other players. I can't lie and say I was consciously being an introvert or single-minded to try and concentrate more on making it but at the same time that was my personality for better or worse. One thing that was real that I definitely didn't need anybody to be telling me was that such and such a player was a great one – I was at Manchester United, after all.

In front of me, Arthur Albiston was breaking into the first team, there was a young lad called Jonathan Clark who got a chance in the team in the November after I joined but aside from that there weren't too many stand-out players. One was Peter

Coyne, a local lad, who could score goals for fun. Martin Rogers was in my year, a left-back from Nottingham, who seemed to be getting opportunities to train and travel with the first team, but apart from him, in my year group, there weren't many who stood out. Andy Ritchie was in the year below; even though there were players in the first team who had come through the youth system, it just seemed to be a period where there weren't too many great young players there who would be challenging those who were already established.

Tommy Docherty was one to give chances but there just weren't players coming through as prolifically as they had under Sir Matt Busby and Jimmy Murphy, real figures of presence who were still at the club. Every time you met them they would always speak pleasantly to you and of you, and they knew who you were. With Sir Matt well into his retirement, we'd tend to see more of Jimmy Murphy who was still working for the club. He'd come to reserve matches and pop his head into the dressing room with the classic line, 'Come on you Red bastards, let's stuff the opposition.'

Years later, Jimmy said one of the most lovely things to me that I kept with me forever. I was in the players' lounge and he came up to me and he said, 'You know something... you'd have been in our team as well.' He'd no need to say that but you can imagine how that made me feel. It still provokes emotion from me today.

People say things like 'he's a Manchester United player' like it's an almost ethereal quality and that's what it felt like Jimmy was saying to me; like I say, he'd no real reason to say it to me but I can still remember his face as he said it. It's something I've treasured since that moment. If you were to say that Manchester United belonged to the identity of one or two people then Sir Matt and Jimmy Murphy would be right at the top of anyone's list, and a compliment like that from someone like Jimmy, who to me *was* and *is* Manchester United, was worth every bit as much as a trophy or a medal.

Back in 1976, having Jimmy Murphy take the time to come down and encourage you to win was all you needed to fire you up before a game. Everyone was aware of who he was and what he'd done. I don't like using the term 'they're like a family' because it's so widely used yet you could see what a community atmosphere they had created at the club. Jimmy and Sir Matt had come from working class backgrounds, had made their way in life and knew what it took. They didn't forget those things and those values that made the club and even though they weren't fully involved, there was an expectancy to follow the tradition and they still did their best to make people feel welcome.

I'd like to think that maybe my own personality and the way I'd been brought up was recognised by the people at the club and that's why I was made so welcome. There are obviously many ingredients which go into making a successful footballer like ability and skill, but looking deeper, ability is just one of many attributes and when you look at each attribute as a component then ability appears to be a very small part of it. Why did players like Jonathan Clark not go on to make it when he seemed talented enough to do so? I'm not saying this is what happened to Jonathan but there are temptations, girls, drink, that kind of lifestyle that is obviously very tempting for a teenage lad and it can be difficult to stay on the straight and narrow. As an apprentice at a Football League club, our first wages were £16 per week, and we were lucky to get that because the year before it had been just £8. A little bit different to today's players who are on high amounts which presents a problem of incentive for managers.

Playing was my motivation and I'd hit the ground running so I did not need any further encouragement to retain my concentration. I was given a chance in the B team after only being at the club for a few weeks. I had signed as a schoolboy throughout the 1975/76 season but that was essentially just an agreement, more like a formality to attach me to the club at the end of the season when I would join as an apprentice. The schoolboy agreement was basically just that, an attachment, we'd get tickets, but as my school still required me to play for them on a Saturday, it was business as usual.

I got into the B team almost straight away in 1976 and it tended to be that if you were full-time at the club you would at least be in that team. You weren't exactly guaranteed a position in the team but you would have cause for concern if you weren't. For me, the B team was great, but I wanted to be in the A team. I'm not pulling it down but the B team seemed an obvious starting place and I wanted to be in the A team as it signalled that you'd made some real progress. It always felt like progress and a commitment at United anyway; the other trials had been days here and there whereas I was now in digs, committed to staying in Manchester even though I still lived local enough to travel in every day if I'd so wished. The atmosphere among the youngsters was good – there was obviously competition and the kind of jokes that go on with young lads but it was good-natured and the lads were all good to get along with.

With my birthday falling quite early in the academic year, I hadn't been on apprentice terms long before I was offered a professional deal on my 17th birthday in September. To outsiders it may have seemed that now I'd joined the club I'd progressed rather rapidly and impressed in a short time to get the deal though I'm certain it was simply down to when my birthday fell; it was commonly accepted that when you got to 17, you would be offered the deal. Nonetheless, it was a great boost to sign as a professional footballer for Manchester United. I'd had a good pre-season with the club after a summer which was one of the hottest on record and I put a stone on in weight – in a good way – through training full-time. There was a milk machine up at The Cliff and after training we'd go through glasses and glasses of it, I'd gone from 9.5st to 10.5st simply through adopting the life of a professional.

Maybe my attitude helped but before long I was playing in the A team – I have to say once again that I don't want to put the B team down. This was my first real taste of representing Manchester United at any level so to play for the B team against proper opposition was a real step up from anything I'd ever known but when you saw a couple of team-mates getting those chances it was only natural to aspire to do the same. There was also another very obvious mantra to consider – if you settled at United, then you weren't going to last long. I hadn't 'made it' because I'd signed professional terms. It would be said to us fairly plainly that we were on the bottom rung and we had to work our way up.

In those early days it was emphasised to us just how hard everyone worked to get the club where it was. There were part-timers like Jimmy Curran and Alan Jones, people who would turn up for the B team to help hand the kit out and act as physios. These were locals who had such a love for the club which shone through and it made it a great place to be; Norman Davies, the ladies in The Cliff's canteen who did the meals for us, an Irish lady named Teresa. There was such a strong community aspect there at that bottom level which brought everything home. Frank Blunstone led the coaching for the youngsters, aided by Jimmy, and he was a really nice bloke. He had worked alongside Tommy Docherty before and was a really bubbly, chirpy personality with an ethos of motivation by encouragement which was very much something that I would respond to.

As players, we understood that whoever we were playing, it was always going to be the cup final for the opposition. Of course there was an obvious pressure to win, but the emphasis for the youth team, the B team and the A team was more about developing and doing things the right way. Playing well and getting beat sometimes was okay. It was okay to lose to a physical team who played long balls as long as you learned and developed; there was an added pressure that came with the FA Youth Cup because you tended to play against better opposition and that was a real chance to test yourself. Frank was a big thinker, he went abroad to watch other clubs and brought ideas back like working with sweepers, etc. It didn't always work, but he was always trying to do something different and evolve.

For me, the encouragement side of it was very positive and something that I would grow to appreciate as a teacher in later life. How can a child of seven or eight make a mistake? They can't, they are simply finding their way. It's the same for younger players. They simply cannot see what older people can see, some things come with height and growth, others with maturity. Frank understood all of these things and was a class act in the way that he handled training and coaching.

There was, however, a negative side to Old Trafford and The Cliff. Tommy Cavanagh, the assistant manager, was very much a ranter and a raver, he could scream and bawl. First-teamers could handle it but the last thing you need as a 16-year-old is knocking down, so as exciting as getting called to train with the first team may be and as envious as you might have been of someone for getting that chance, you certainly didn't envy that they would be in the firing line of Tommy Cav! It was such a symbolic step; we didn't even change with the first team, our changing room was down the other end, and the changing room had three stages of development which marked your progression. I've thought about it a lot and I don't think that Cav did it to test a personality or the strength of character, I think it was just in his nature and the way that he was. Did he want a reaction? I don't know, I just know that if he had a go at me, I would try and get on with things rather than dwell too much on it. It was never pleasant but I felt the best way to deal with it was rise above it and prove myself with performances.

It's interesting from a psychological perspective to wonder how and why that type of coaching is effective, as it was something that was continued at the club under Eric Harrison when he brought through that first group of talented players at United in 1992. It may well be to test character but then you could say that those who make it through such a system were always going to make it anyway, no matter what; the more aggressive approach may well have broken the spirit or character of plenty of players who were talented enough but just couldn't hack it. Maybe the tough love had a negative effect on some who may have regressed because of that pressure. Luckily for me, I was able to handle it.

Our first big test came in the FA Youth Cup against Bolton Wanderers at Burnden Park and it was a disappointing game. We'd played Southport previously at Old Trafford and it was abandoned because the fog was so thick that we couldn't see from one end to the other. It was farcical that it was allowed to continue as long as it did, but we won the replay to come up against Bolton. They were a physical side, more physical than us and we never really got going. An exit almost straight away was disappointing of course but I can't recall anyone having a go at us, even Cav! We were told it was going to be tough, that it was Bolton's cup final, and that was a bit of a learning curve for us. I wouldn't say it was an added pressure but it was something we learned, some experience for us to take under our belt and we knew it was going to be the same for every team. You know at United that you have to be on your game every week but when you're so young it can take you aback just how much people raise their game to play against you and it's something you have to learn to handle very quickly. Otherwise, like we found out against Bolton, it could mean an early exit.

I suppose it's a natural thing that teams would be more competitive against Manchester United than against any other team but that was simply something we'd have to deal with every week. For us as players, we just had to accept that that was the kind of thing we'd come up against. We hadn't seen those players before, we didn't know what their natural performance levels were like and so the only thing we could do was play to the best of our ability and try and beat what was in front of us. It was a valuable education; it was something that had been told to us by the coaches but when you are experiencing it on the pitch that's when you know that you have to make sure you're always giving your maximum.

Defeat in the FA Youth Cup didn't hamper my progression. That progression included annual participation in the Blue Star tournament which was held over in Switzerland. I can still remember the Hotel Stoller, a great base for us, that served the best strawberries and cream ever. The Blue Star was a prestigious tournament and offered an early exposure into continental football and what came with it. I felt I'd done all right in the various competitions; I made it into the A team and then after the turn of 1976 I began to get some opportunities in the reserves. I was playing at centre-half – it was funny, as I'd been a centre-forward at school, and I moved back into midfield which is where I played when I joined the club but then I'd moved further back again. Maybe they were telling me something!

I'm not being big-headed but I didn't feel as if I'd struggled against anyone; I had bad games, I can't deny that, but those were games in which I felt I'd struggled for my own reasons rather than what an opponent had done. In fact, I thought I'd done well against certain players and maybe that was noticed by the coaches and brought about my progression. When I was playing in the Central League in the reserve team it was a whole new experience.

The B and A teams are usually made up of players like yourself, clamouring for that opportunity at a higher level, but the reserves are a different thing altogether. There are players like yourself, youngsters who've made the step up, but also first-team players coming back from injury or players on the periphery of the first team. And they would be good players, when you consider that there was only one substitute allowed to be named. It was a good mix and a really competitive environment for a youngster and I still felt I was giving a good account of myself. That was until I came up against a lad who I wasn't aware of at the time, against Liverpool. I thought, 'He's not bad, this lad can play.' It was the first time I'd come up against someone and really thought I'd been in a tough game and it turned out to be a young player called Ian Rush, who they'd just signed from Chester City. I wonder what became of him?!

I felt that being exposed to that more senior environment at the tender age of 17 was the best thing for my development. It's what you strive for, to be playing with the first-team players and it's great to be given that chance. Things have changed these days with the bigger squads and the under-21 league and what's good for one player isn't necessarily good for another; for me, it felt okay, I didn't feel out of place. That said, I felt I was moving at the right pace. I didn't feel as if the speed of my progression meant that I should be challenging for a spot in the first team already, that was way too far ahead and I was able to see that first hand when some of us would be called in to play against the senior players in training. When one of the older players was injured, then one of the kids would be drafted in to play for the senior team in training and that was sort of the next step – you could see that you would be able to get a chance to impress and the coaches were able to see how you played alongside these players in a controlled environment.

United had enjoyed a great season in 1976/77 and had got to Wembley again for the FA Cup Final to face Liverpool. With the game approaching and a slight fixture pile-up, there was some squad rotation yet I honestly never expected or believed I would get a chance. Nor was I led to believe I would. As I say, everything so far had felt right, and maybe the leap into first-team football would have been too much for me. Not in a footballing sense. I'm sure I could have held my own with that, I was confident enough in my own ability. But the other side of it was still something I was coming to terms with, and maybe that wasn't helped by the fact that I'd played with so many different teams that I never really had a settled run of team-mates to get to know.

I did get to go to the cup final again, with John McDermott, a fellow young player who actually would go on to be the best man at my wedding. We had won the award for United's two best apprentices of the year and we got a trip down to the league game against West Ham with the first team. It was the last league game of the season, and it was such an eye-opening experience for John and myself. We travelled down on the train, the hotel was really nice and it was good to see how the club operated on that level. After the game, the first team stayed and moved into the hotel where they would prepare for the cup final. John and I travelled back with Norman Davies with big wicker baskets filled with the kits and we cleaned the players' boots at Old Trafford. We normally did it in the boot room but for some reason we did it on the pitch that day under beautiful sunshine. Sadly we didn't get to go back down with it – Norman collected it all and went back to London. I remember John and I having a big argument about who had cleaned Jimmy Greenhoff and Lou Macari's boots – it was almost as controversial as who had scored the winner in the game itself! It was good that I got to experience that with John, a player of my own age that I was able to talk to. The older players did try and involve us and talk to us but that was more a polite thing – it was a nice taster for us to see that side of first-team football.

Everybody from the club went down to Wembley on the Saturday morning of the game. Everybody! There were so many coaches outside Old Trafford; dad took my granddad as he'd never been to an FA Cup Final before; they drove, and I went down with the other youngsters in the coach. We stopped at lunchtime for a meal and then getting there for the game itself was brilliant, United beating Liverpool to win the cup. Just like the Southampton game, I was involved yet not involved. Compared to the previous year, it was slightly more intense with the identity of the opponent taken into consideration. There were few nerves, just excitement about the occasion. It was a great feeling to be involved as part of the club after such a victorious day and we managed to stay with the team for the after party – I can't remember if everyone from the club managed to stay, but we certainly did – and we were lucky enough to get our pictures taken with the cup after Brian Greenhoff kindly sorted that out. I was surprised to see that picture pop up in Brian's own autobiography!

Just to be among it was an incredible feeling, the perfect end to a year where I felt I'd been on the crest of a wave. It was enough to whet your appetite and think, 'This is what I want, this is where I want to be.' Liverpool were doing what United would go on to do in the 1990s and 2000s so it was a big statement of intent of what we could do in the future.

To be fair, I hadn't had too much personal involvement with Tommy Docherty (our interaction would almost always be with

Frank Blunstone), but once the news broke that he'd had an affair with the wife of the physiotherapist, I struggled to see how he could remain at Manchester United. If he was to remain at the club, how could I believe in anything he saw or said? How could I go to him with confidence he was being truthful and not disloyal? Perhaps the club saw it the same way. There was no doubting he was a popular manager among some of the players; Brian, Lou Macari, Sammy McIlroy, Stuart Pearson, these players had had a great time with The Doc, they'd grown up together as a team and played some absolutely fantastic football. There would never be many 0-0s with that team. Maybe they'd have liked to have seen him stay but for me, the club made the right decision, and maybe the only decision that could really have been made in order to preserve the identity of the club.

I don't want to go into the rights and wrongs of what Tommy did but an event like that was so cataclysmic within the club that it may have forced people to take sides – I didn't have that much contact with him before, I can't comment on the controversies that followed the relationships and allegations with other people. Looking forward, and it's only my personal opinion, I couldn't see how I could go to him in confidence as a professional.

Opinions are one thing, fact is another, and Tommy Docherty was no longer manager of Manchester United. The potential of that side has been debated since, what they might have achieved if United had signed Peter Shilton, but the same could be said of the team under Dave Sexton or Ron Atkinson. And certainly, Peter's name would come up for discussion again.

Hindsight's a great thing isn't it – I can't say for certain what would have happened but I can only say what I believe and be it for the 1976 team or the teams I played in, Peter Shilton would have been a hell of a signing for Manchester United. He was the best around and I feel you might have been able to compare his impact to that made by Peter Schmeichel when he arrived at United. If we'd have had someone of that stature it would have made a big difference. Brian Clough came out with a famous quote that Shilton was worth ten to 15 points for Forest every season and that was something that could well be fair. When you take a second to reflect on the enormity of that statement, even when it was two points for a win, it might have meant the wait for a league championship wouldn't have been anywhere near as long as what it was.

Peter wouldn't be coming to Old Trafford but there were plenty of new faces coming in, and some inevitable departures after Tommy was sacked. Frank Blunstone was one of those who left while Tommy Cav stayed on; Joe Brown came from Burnley to run the youth team while Paddy Crerand seemed to take a more prominent role. Under the new management, although we wouldn't sign Shilton, we did have a legendary goalkeeping presence return to the club in the shape of Harry Gregg to do some coaching. I don't think Harry lasted long because of his very strong personality! There was a little bit of instability with the younger players in the immediate aftermath of Tommy's departure which was at odds with the new manager's apparent intention, which at least on the face of it seemed to be to instil tradition and continuity with the re-introduction of older faces at the club.

That new manager was Dave Sexton. To be perfectly honest I didn't know anything about him so I was unable to make a judgement on whether I thought it was the right or wrong appointment. He was a pleasant, mild-mannered man who was quietly spoken but very articulate. For me, although I think the word 'refreshing' might be a bit too far, I certainly welcomed the change in personality from the bold and in-your-face style of The Doc. The biggest problem Dave faced in the early days was that Cav was still there; that might seem a little bit harsh, but particularly for some of the younger lads, they – and I – thought he might have left with The Doc. It wouldn't be false to say there was perhaps a little disappointment that Cav had remained at the club. Nine times out of ten when a new manager takes over he brings his own backroom staff – you only have to look at what happened with Sir Alex Ferguson retiring and David Moyes making a whole heap of changes.

Although I wasn't able to cast a strong enough opinion on him, there was some reservation that Dave Sexton wouldn't be as cavalier as Tommy Docherty – when you look at the Queens Park Rangers team that Dave managed before arriving at United, you'd have to say that it was an unfair accusation, as they were certainly entertaining. I felt at ease under and around Dave – other players had different views because of his studious nature. Tommy would trust in the players to go out and play but Dave was a little more tactical in his preparation and such a profound change isn't always welcomed by some individuals who are used to playing a certain way.

First-team politics was not something that interested me or anything I was likely to get involved with. In the 1976/77 season I'd made the step from the B team, to the A team, to the reserves, and my ambition for the new season under the new management was simply to make sure I got a regular place in the reserves. I'd played most often at centre-half but had been used in midfield and at full-back as well – I was just happy to be playing. I wasn't the kind of person who would cause a fuss because I was playing in a certain position; I'd rather be on the pitch in any position than off of it and I felt fortunate enough that my form was good enough to justify a run in the team.

Later on in my career Ray Wilkins said to me that I lost out on specialising in a position because of my willingness to play in a number of roles; it does make sense, yet at the time it doesn't matter to you as you're just happy to be playing. In retrospect I can certainly see what he was saying and I can see how that might have hindered me. On the other hand, being able to play in a number of positions was maybe one of the reasons I played so many times for United in the future. If you're stuck with the tag of being versatile, for better or worse, how *do* you change it? If you're good at playing in certain positions and people see that, the chances are you'll be played in those roles. I wouldn't like to say you're being used or taken advantage of and like I said it was certainly not something I thought about at the time. I suppose it's like the ultimate back-handed compliment, really. But what was I going to do? As a 16- or 17-year-old, turn around and say, 'No, I'm a centre-half!' That would take some doing, and I wouldn't have done that at any age. Play poorly deliberately to avoid getting selected there again? No chance.

Through the majority of the 1977/78 season there was no chance that versatility would be a problem as I managed to play often at centre-half – in fact, the demon I did face was my appendix. I was in good form so it came at a bad time, but I was able to recover from that and get my place in the team again. As the season wore on, I was satisfied with my own development but there had been a subtle change in the way that the first team seemed to be bringing through youngsters.

Tommy Docherty would often call up two or three kids to be around the squad on matchday whereas Dave was nowhere near as prolific; the odd one might have been selected here and there. Andy Ritchie was in the year below me and he'd jumped ahead, being involved with the first team on a regular basis – the opportunity was there, but it didn't seem as regular. You could look at that both ways, though. If the youngsters aren't good enough to challenge what you've got, then why put them in? Was Dave being unfairly criticised for not bringing youth players through – and with the same logic, was Tommy Docherty getting a lot of praise for bringing through the likes of Sammy McIlroy and Brian Greenhoff, when in reality they'd been brought to the club by Sir Matt Busby? It seemed as if there were a lot under Tommy, but maybe that wasn't actually the case after Arthur Albiston and Jimmy Nicholl.

Towards the end of the season I was given my first taste of senior football when I was called into the squad for David Sadler's testimonial game at Preston. When I was told I was going to be included I was so nervous – I think I was the only youngster to have been called up, so I knew I would be on my own. That was always going to be the tough part for me, going to the ground and getting on the coach. Once you get to the ground everything starts to change and that's what it was like for me at Deepdale. I got to the changing room and started sorting my kit out and I was able to get my mentality in check. Like I say, it wasn't the fault of the older players, they would do their best to include me, but from my side it was something that was difficult. There's little you can do to control it and you're sort of left to dwell on it by yourself so you need to create some form of tunnel vision. I was named as substitute and when I came on, for Gordon McQueen, it was more of a relief than anything else!

To get out on the pitch and shed myself of the nerves of the build-up was something that was most welcome. Be it six people or 60,000, for whatever reason, I wasn't usually prone to nerves once I was on the pitch, as that's where I wanted to be. Testimonials can be ten a penny these days but it was great to commemorate the service of David Sadler to United; I'd never met him before but I knew of his contribution to the club and it was an honour to be included both for the game and the meal afterwards. Following that, it was back in the reserves for me to conclude the 1977/78 season, which was ultimately an underwhelming one for the club on the back of the FA Cup-winning campaign.

I was, however, involved in the post-season trip to Scandinavia. You might think that with the way I've built it up that it would be my worst nightmare and it was tough but I was able to room with Jonathan Clark who was taken too; it was sensible for me to be with someone of my own age, and he'd been around the first team quite often too so knew the routines. It was a struggle of a trip; we turned up at Old Trafford on the morning to go and all of the other players were dressed in a club top and matching tracksuit bottoms, and I hadn't been given any, for some reason. I was wearing a shirt and trousers, and then Tommy Cav had a go at me asking me why I wasn't wearing my club blazer. I wasn't even told! At the age of 18 I didn't know what was expected of me, I hadn't been told and I wasn't a mind-reader.

At the airport I stood out like a sore thumb – with Martin Rogers, who I think had forgotten his stuff – and that didn't help. Once we were out there and training, that was fine and no problem, but you know that after that you're going to have to go to the hotel and be expected to socialise. It was enjoyable in so much as I saw different places and people and it was a proud thing to be representing the club abroad, another learning process that I was getting something from, another step in the right direction. The difficulties that came as part of the package were just something I was going to have to learn to deal with.

With the 1978/79 season under way and with two seasons of development at the club, honestly, I had hoped that I would be in contention for the senior team. I felt I was doing well but I wasn't even travelling with the first team. I'd become a regular in the Central League but as the season closed and a new one came in, I began to feel some frustration. As I approached my 20th birthday in 1979, I started to think for the first time that something ought to happen soon or I might have to consider my long-term future at the club.

It could hardly be said I was a late bloomer as I'd made such progression in my first two seasons at the club but the last one had seen me just ticking along, not really getting anywhere, and with that being the same way going into my fourth year at the club it began to feel more like it was stalling. I was wondering if I'd have to go on loan, or if I'd not even be offered a contract. After witnessing two FA Cup finals, I confess that from a selfish point of view I was disappointed that I'd not even been considered in the build-up to the 1979 FA Cup Final. To not be involved or even in the squad felt like a setback; it was a letdown that we were beaten, but selfishly, I was more upset that I'd not been in contention.

With the manner of the defeat, though, maybe the players on the day had more cause to be disappointed. It was a flat feeling around the club after that game and that was certainly something I felt.

That underwhelming feeling continued when I was selected for another England youth trial down at Lilleshall; I didn't expect to be asked, to be fair. I don't know why – maybe it's because I thought I hadn't moved forward, as such, at United. It was nice to be asked but maybe because of that lack of ultimate confidence in myself and, again, the fact it was three days away from my home comforts with people I didn't know, I was not entirely thrilled to be travelling and mixing with them. It should have been something I looked forward to and, moving forward it would certainly be part of my education, yet with everything the way it was, I have to say I wasn't that surprised when I missed out on selection again.

I'm not making excuses, they didn't pick me and I didn't feel I'd expressed myself particularly well, so if they were going to choose based on what they'd seen they would have no reason to select me. I can't help but feel that inhibition held me back and counted against me.

I had two choices in the summer of 1979, to wilt under the pressure or stand up and give it another chance. I was never going to give up that opportunity and so resolved to continue as I had been; working hard and trying to show with my performances that I was good enough. And then I started to get small glimpses, glimmers of hope, small indications of progression. I'd find myself training with the first team on a more regular basis, though I would never be in contention for a position in the squad at the end of the week. It was not a lot, but it was great, it was just enough encouragement to keep the hope alive. Maybe it was a pivotal event, if it hadn't been that way, I might have given up. Even though there wasn't that game, there was now a sign of progression.

At the time, there was an obvious frustration that I had felt that was not being eased but with the benefit of hindsight I can look at things and think that things worked out for the best. Maybe exposing me to senior football earlier wouldn't have helped when taking into consideration all the other problems I'd faced with my development and integration. I wasn't jealous of Andy Ritchie, who was now getting regular first-team football and scoring goals, but I was envious of him. And when I looked at the team, who were doing really well, I could understand why I wasn't in the first team at that point – they were challenging at the top of the table, had a strong centre-half partnership in Martin Buchan and Gordon McQueen, and with Jimmy Nicholl and Arthur Albiston in the full-back positions, Dave Sexton had a back line which he trusted.

Dave had brought in Gordon McQueen in 1978 and it immediately made me feel a bit uneasy because it was my position and then when Kevin Moran was brought in and given his debut towards the end of the 1978/79 season I began to wonder if my opportunity would come at all. It was competitive but there was a great blend in the dressing room; Gordon would like a laugh and a joke whereas Martin would have his moments. He was a superb captain and led by example; I would take in all of their advice, and they would give plenty. That went around the dressing room – I'm running the risk of repeating myself too much here but if there was a problem on that side of things, it was from my side and the problems that I had feeling comfortable. Maybe that's the wrong turn of phrase, I just found it hard work. The 1979/80 season concluded with United failing to win the league on the final day after failing to win at Leeds; I wasn't there, but I think the chances were remote anyway due to the superior goal average Liverpool had.

Still, it was two defeats in two competitions in two years that had gone right down to the wire – it was enough vindication in Dave Sexton that he was moving in the right direction with United. The difference in atmosphere that is generated with a league run compared to one in a cup competition is noticeable; the cup is one game at a time and you only really talk about it around the time of the games or when you're preparing, but when it was the league, it was something that was on the lips of everyone from people in the media to people at The Cliff; we hadn't won the title since 1967 and to come fairly close, the closest we'd been since, was encouraging.

United had come on and for me, the challenge was to do the same. It had felt like two or three years in the same position; I'd remained in digs in Davyhulme, and the only real changes to my personal life were that I'd started seeing Karen and passed my driving test, so I was spending all my weekends back home. I'd known Karen's family for a few years previously, but mainly through her brothers and her sister Tracey who was a big friend of my elder sister Anne. The Entwistle family lived literally the length of three football fields away from our house but it wasn't until I started going down to Hyndburn Sports Centre that I really noticed Karen. She was working part-time in the cafeteria and after a couple of false starts I became brave enough to ask her out.

At 20, I was an adult, and I'd started looking at things more positively when thinking of my first-team chances. You can imagine my dismay, then, when I didn't feature in a single pre-season game heading into the 1980/81 season. For the first time, seriously, I was forced to contemplate whether my career at Manchester United would be over before it'd had a chance to begin.

3

'There are many ways of going forward, but only one way of standing still.'

Franklin D. Roosevelt

I WASN'T ever going to agitate for a move away from Manchester United but it's only natural that the thought crosses your mind if you've had two years of slow progress. In the pre-season of 1980/81 I felt as far away as I'd ever been from getting a chance as I didn't get a minute with the senior team, nor was I included in the reckoning for the First Division opener against Middlesbrough.

I wouldn't have asked to leave permanently but it was certainly getting to the stage where I would have felt bold enough or frustrated enough to enquire about the opportunity of a loan move. No-one wants to leave Manchester United, I don't care what they say, but as a professional at the age of almost 21, nobody wants to languish in the reserves for the entirety of their career. Late on in his career Michael Owen said publicly that he would have preferred to be on the bench at Manchester United than in the first team elsewhere; maybe he was at the point in his career where that was something he could settle for, but I'm not certain he would have felt the same if it had been at the start of his career. I must admit it's an attitude I've never been familiar with at any point; I was never happy to be a substitute, my own mentality has always been that I wanted to play, otherwise I don't know why you're in the sport!

Not that I felt my destiny was purely in my hands; I had concerns that I was not wanted, too, so I was half-expecting to be told that an offer had come in and I would be on my way. I certainly didn't hear of anything concrete; there were one or two rumours that it would be it for me if I was not to break in soon. For whatever reason it didn't happen and I'm grateful for that.

Everybody wants to be at United but in those days it was 11 on the pitch and one substitute – nowadays there are players of 20 or 21 who are nowhere near the matchday squads which have 18 or 19 players that can be named and of course, you feel sympathy for them, but with the way the game has moved on they know what they're getting into – the statistics are there to prove just how slim the chances are of progression through the ranks; everybody is striving to be that one who makes the breakthrough which just reinforces how difficult it is. I did have one phone call to me personally asking whether I would be interested in a move away but I was adamant that I was going to be that one that did make it at United so I refused it with no consideration.

When I used to go to my cousin's on a weekend, my auntie would say to me, 'You know there's only one in a thousand who become a professional footballer.' I wasn't one for rash statements, I don't suppose I ever have been, but I turned around, looked her in the eye and said to her, 'I'm gonna be that one.' Why I said it, I haven't got a clue, but there must have been some inner belief and resolve.

Even the strongest of characters might have felt close to breaking point as the Middlesbrough game and then a defeat at Wolverhampton Wanderers went by with me seemingly no closer.

I don't know what triggered the events, I can't remember any injuries, but out of the blue I was called into the squad for the following game against Birmingham City at St Andrew's. It was great to be called up – I didn't have any inkling leading up to it that I would be named in the squad even when I travelled with them, right up until an hour before kick-off when Dave Sexton named his team. Considering how nerves can fester and eat away at you, I think it was better to know an hour before than the night before. With an hour's notice you can go straight into your zone and block everything out without having to dwell on it, and particularly when it came to my first inclusion in the squad, that was the best for me.

With the way I was as a person and the way I prepared for a game, I found that operating within that tunnel vision was the best, or perhaps only, way I could comfortably prepare. As a youngster breaking into the first team it certainly was as I didn't know any of my new team-mates on a personal basis – you knew them, of course, but there is a difference between being a young kid from the reserves and someone making your first steps as one of 'them'. Later in my career, with future managers, the teamsheet would go up as early as Friday lunchtime and even then I'd immediately go into a zone where I'd block everything out. That's something I'll go into more detail with a little later.

It's never nice when a team-mate is injured but a crisis for one presents an opportunity for another and that was the case when Kevin Moran picked up a knock at Birmingham – it was enough to bring him off with the entire second half left to play. That was better for me, too, I didn't just have a couple of minutes, I had a real opportunity to get into my stride. I knew it was going to be a real test at centre-half as I was up against Frank Worthington, an experienced centre-forward who had scored goals for Huddersfield, Leicester, and Bolton before going to Birmingham and had even played and scored for England, too. It was probably for the best that Frank wasn't an overly physical player as there were a fair few robust players of that type around. I felt I'd done okay – it was very difficult to get used to the pace, though. You hear people talk about that but nothing can prepare you for the jump from practice, training and reserve games to the pace of a game at the highest level.

Another difficulty that immediately jumped out at me was how the atmosphere had such an effect on the ability to communicate with a team-mate. You'd shout to someone but the noise was so great that it felt as if it was getting lost. The pace and noise were things I was going to have to learn to control, and it got easier over time, but it was very difficult in the first few games. Having been sat among the United supporters when they were at their most intense and raucous, I was still taken aback by just how deafening the atmosphere could be once you crossed the line.

After the Birmingham City match I played at Anfield for the reserves and I got a whack midway through the game. I'm not a naturally pessimistic person but I thought, 'Goodness me!'

I'd got involved, finally, pushed my way there and earned my spot in the first team finally and then this happened. It was only a knock but enough to keep me out of the team for two weeks and enough to make me wonder if that was my chance gone. I wasn't down, or depressed, but I was frustrated while injured. Thankfully, on my return I was back training with the first team so I had an indication things would be all right.

I could never say that playing for Manchester United was an inconvenience but the next game I would play was against

Tottenham Hotspur at White Hart Lane on the weekend after my 21st birthday. In the pre-season I'd looked through the fixture list of the reserve team to tentatively make plans for the occasion and United were at home so we booked a party at a local venue. Then I get called up for one of the longest trips we could possibly have! I would again come on as substitute in a 0-0 draw away from home but the thing that once again stuck out to me was the atmosphere – 40,000 screaming supporters and I was wondering how the hell I was going to get used to it. I don't know if any of the intimidation was to do with the stadium itself; a point was a decent result to be coming away with from Spurs, though.

Afterwards, I was keen to get back home as soon as possible. Not only had we got to get back to Old Trafford but then I had to travel another three-quarters of an hour to Accrington where we were living. I think, when I finally got there, it was 10.30pm – there were a lot of people there, a lot of people I went to school with and a lot that I hadn't seen for a long while. It wasn't an all-nighter – I think it lasted until around 1am. I felt a bit like the Queen in a way, going around and speaking to everyone! The change in attention that you get when you become a Manchester United first-teamer is immediate and sudden.

I was always going to get attention at my 21st birthday party but it still surprises you how everyone wants to talk to you all of a sudden. I can remember being outside Old Trafford doing a press interview in those early days and a lot of supporters gathering around and asking for my autograph. To be recognised in just a week after being essentially anonymous was yet another thing I was going to have to get used to! I wasn't annoyed or anything – how could I be, I fully understood what it was like to be a supporter – but I did feel uncomfortable with being noticed.

One time Karen and I were walking through Accrington and there was some guy across the road and I could feel him staring but we just continued to walk; he shouted 'Mick!' which caused Karen to turn her head and look at him but I just wanted to walk on. Call it adulation, call it whatever you want, but I always felt a little embarrassed about it. Not least because when I was in the team there was always a Sammy McIlroy, a Bryan Robson, an established star with a different status. I knew it was never going to get stupid or as crazy as the attention that they got, so in a way that kind of helped me appreciate it a little bit more.

These days the club do much to prepare the youngsters for the kind of attention they face and many of them are treated like idols before they even play for the first team. Back in 1980 we were left to our own devices; when you come off a pitch and you're in the heat of the moment with adrenalin pumping and then someone sticks a microphone under your nose expecting a quote you've got to be very careful. If you've been brought off or disagreed with a decision from the manager, you can't have a go at them as you'll get yourself into bother.

There are two ways of looking at it, though. Yes, I suppose it's a good thing to prepare youngsters and not have them caught by surprise, but then there's the other side where almost every interview is the same, there are a bunch of stereotypical answers, the stock quotes that are given to stock questions. People talk about that being a reason why there seems to be a lack of characters in today's game but I think, to be fair, that was something that was said about the generation before when I was playing, too. Either way, you can see, understand and appreciate the reasons why clubs do train their players to handle the press, even if that has made it sterile in the opinions of some.

When you turn 21 you're officially an adult, a man, but the difference in my life in those few days had been remarkable and was going to take some getting used to. One new experience that

I was definitely looking forward to was my first match at Old Trafford and 11 days after that Spurs game and my birthday party, I was given it. There can hardly be a bad way to make your first appearance at Old Trafford but a midweek European game must be high up on the list. I'd experienced them and wanted to be part of it – and even though I was delighted to come on as substitute again, I was itching to get the kind of feeling that must come with starting such a game. I felt, once again, that I'd acquitted myself okay, against opponents in Widzew Lodz that weren't the most famous team but certainly provided stern competition. McIlroy scored in a 1-1 draw which meant we were up against it in the second leg. We ought to have won in Poland, we had a few chances where we hit the post, but sadly it wasn't to be and we were eliminated on away goals after a scoreless draw.

Between the two legs I had made my full debut for the club. You couldn't call away games at Birmingham and Spurs a gentle introduction to first-team football but they weren't as hostile as my next two league games. The first was at Leeds where I would come on as substitute again – for the fourth consecutive match. I roomed with Jimmy Greenhoff, the former Leeds player, and I think it helped me to be with a senior player who was used to both sides of that particular coin. When I was named as substitute, I always knew I would get a chance with about ten minutes left. Elland Road must have been volatile but there was nothing remarkable in another goalless draw. Travelling with the squad and being included may well have been that 'natural progression' I spoke of earlier yet with all the trappings that came with it, it did seem a more profound step and so, with the benefit of hindsight, the chance coming at 21 when I was more prepared to deal with it was for the best.

4

Big Changes

IT was always the way that we'd train at The Cliff all week and then on a Friday morning we'd train at Old Trafford where we'd have a five-a-side on about a quarter of the pitch, a nice and easy session ahead of the game on Saturday. Ahead of the Manchester derby in September 1980 I'd arrived at Old Trafford and had begun to get changed in the dressing room when Dave Sexton came in and said, 'Don't bother training today, just leave it, you've done enough this week,' and never said anything else.

I had an inkling, then, that I might be involved from the start against City. Was he wrapping me in cotton wool? Maybe so… but Dave was aware of my character, and I thought, surely he wouldn't leave me with this long to think about it? After training a few of the lads were asking why I hadn't trained – I said I didn't know, but they were certain that it meant I was going to play. At that time, before home games, Dave used to take us up to Mottram Hall on a Friday night. That was great for me as a young lad though maybe not so much for the older players with wives and families. On second thoughts, maybe they liked that!

I would normally eat at Mrs Williams's house and she would cook really well for us. It would be a three-course job, soup or fruit, then maybe a main of chop and chips, and a pudding of ice cream. I ate there about 5pm and then went to meet the team at Old Trafford at 6pm, where we'd all go to Mottram together. Once there and settled in the room, we'd come back down for an evening meal. I'd eat that one, too! I'd try and eat something a bit lighter, prawns and fish or something like that.

That was a routine that went on for a while, I've no idea why I didn't just say to the landlady, 'No, it's okay, we'll be having something to eat later.' I told Stevie Coppell about it, and then Lou Macari got hold of it as well. They would joke about saying that I could play, and eat, for England! I did love my food, I was fortunate in that I could eat what I wanted and not seem to put weight on.

That night I managed to have a really good sleep. I think I was sharing a room with Mickey Thomas. I must have had a good night's sleep if Mickey didn't bother me! In the morning we travelled to Old Trafford and had our pre-match meal in the Grill Room. It was a regular thing for footballers of the time to have a steak – three hours before a match. I had mine rare with the thinking that it would dissolve better, but I don't think you'd be allowed anywhere near anything like that these days.

Before the match we went down to the players' lounge where some of them were watching *Grandstand* on the BBC. At 2pm we went into the changing room and discovered the team – this was before shirts had names on them, so it wasn't as if you'd know as soon as you walked in. The teamsheet was read out and I was at number ten, a centre-forward's number normally, but I was to play in midfield. I was nervous but prepared the way I had been doing as a substitute, taking my shirt and tie off and then doing my own warm-up in the changing room. At ten to three the bell went and we went and prepared to line up in the tunnel. This was when the teams came out on the halfway line – prior to coming out, you couldn't really tell what the atmosphere would be like.

It was a strange tunnel, as well – I know it's still in operation for stadium tours, and you can observe the strange slope as it comes out. It was a nightmare to walk on with aluminium studs! If you set off running you had to keep running with the momentum, but momentum and adrenalin was very much something that I was feeling the first time I did that run out to play in the Manchester derby. The roar as we left the tunnel was extraordinary.

I was always proud to wear any number for Manchester United but a number between two and 11 was significant and meant so much – it didn't matter what number it was as long as I was starting. I was nervous but fortunate to be surrounded by class players with bags of experience – the likes of Arthur and Martin who'd been there time and time before, who congratulated me and wished me good luck but also reassured me by saying I'd be fine if I played my natural game, and told me to try my best to enjoy it. To be in among people who had been through that same system like Arthur and Sammy was great and to have that kind of advice was brilliant.

We kicked off and often in a game of football you'll see that the forwards kick off and it usually goes straight back to a midfielder – that's what happened to me and I suppose it seems fairly insignificant from the outside but I remember it so vividly as being a moment that could have made me or broken me. I received the ball immediately and turned; I felt under pressure from Steve Daley, the expensive signing City had made, and I just dragged the ball back – Steve went whizzing past and I was able to just lay it off comfortably to Jimmy Nicholl. from that, everything seemed to go right – I could feel confident and grow in that confidence as well. Things seemed to go really well, my tackles were well timed and my passes were okay. I laid the first goal on for Stevie Coppell, whose initial shot was saved but he put the rebound in. The celebrations that followed that goal were brilliant, to have contributed was fantastic – I think I just went mad on my own!

Late on, I started to feel tired as you would. Someone smashed the ball and it hit me in the face which shook me up but I managed to get myself together until cramp started to settle in. We were 2-1 up with about ten minutes left when I could physically not continue and I was brought off – Tom Sloan, a young Irish player on the fringes of the squad, came on for what would be his penultimate appearance for the club and, exhausted, I headed straight for the dressing room to try and get a bit of physio. Playing in midfield for United means you're always going to be called upon to be active but I would have probably run my socks off if I'd been wearing the goalkeeper's jersey I was so keen – most of my substitute appearances had been in midfield so I felt comfortable there.

Until the lads came back in I wasn't aware it had finished 2-2, as City had snatched an equaliser late on – that meant my record in the first team was five appearances and five draws, a run that continued as I kept my place for the return game against Lodz. It was a case of lucky number seven all round as I wore that shirt at Nottingham Forest in my first win with the senior side. That said, a draw wasn't a bad result, especially as it was only two points for a win then. We saw it as a positive that we were on an unbeaten run and it was most definitely a positive to come away from the City Ground with both points against Forest who were enjoying a golden period in their history under Brian Clough.

Brian was one of the game's most colourful and controversial characters. He was always pleasant with me and I'd always heard good stories about him prior to meeting him. He was the type to come in to your dressing room before the game and wish you good luck – it was unheard of for an opposing manager to do that at the time. I don't suppose it's that common now either. As a matter of fact I can't really recount any bad stories of Brian – after I made my England debut a couple of years later, he said that he'd seen me play against him at Forest and he was impressed with me. As with the words that Jimmy Murphy had said to me, it was something that really made an impression on me, particularly so given Brian's reputation – it's that side of people that some outsiders don't get to see and it certainly meant a lot to me.

After 12 games in the First Division in 1980/81 we'd lost only once but drawn eight times – maybe some of our players were looking at the pools! Draws against Aston Villa and Arsenal at Old Trafford and then at Ipswich put us in seventh on 14 points but it emphasises the point about those draws not being poor results as Ipswich, who were top, only had 18 points themselves. For whatever reason we had not managed to put results to bed but looking at the team I couldn't say that we were lacking in any particular area – the league was simply that competitive that all the top teams would tend to take points off each other, and to turn it around the other way, it showed how difficult we were to beat ourselves.

One thing you could not accuse us of was complacency. I'd hate for anyone to have said that to me, as I knew how hard I'd worked to get into the position I was in, and I could say the same for the other lads too. Maybe the pressure of almost 15 years without a league title at the club was part of it but then every game at United came with that pressure and expectancy. It was always going to be the case that other teams saw us as their big fixture, the one their fans would be up for if they came to Old Trafford and the one guaranteed sell-out at their own stadium. As we'd finished second the previous season, we'd become a scalp in terms of quality rather than just the name as well. Because I'd come through the ranks I was used to it at every level and was well aware of the need to ensure we were at our best every game.

When you look through Sir Alex's reign, whenever there was a need to make a statement or come back from a disappointment, more often than not that would be made by signing a striker. Andy Cole, Dwight Yorke, Ruud van Nistelrooy, Wayne Rooney, Robin van Persie – all of these were statement signings that were either made from a position of strength or to provide an extra dimension. A team can work well together but strikers obviously cause problems for the opposition and maybe that was something on Dave Sexton's mind following those draws. I don't think we were lacking a cutting edge but Dave made what I think he hoped would be a huge statement of intent when he signed Garry Birtles from Nottingham Forest for £1.25m. Garry had won two European Cups and a First Division title with Forest and I thought it was an absolutely great buy. Every time I saw him he was either scoring goals or proving to be a handful and I'm sure that everyone thought he was certain to be a success.

For one reason or another that sadly didn't happen for Garry and only he would really be able to tell you why; he was a lovely lad and settled in great, he and his young wife settled into the area. There were others who didn't exactly settle, or didn't have everything in place, but Garry definitely seemed to have everything set up for him to succeed at Old Trafford. And, performance-wise, he did okay. But as a centre-forward, particularly one of expense, you have to be scoring goals. The longer it went on for him without hitting the net, the more difficult it became, he was trying harder and then when everything becomes an effort you can see signs of struggle.

He certainly started well enough, helping the team to consecutive wins in his first two games against Stoke City and Everton. But then it wasn't just Garry who was struggling as we went three games without a goal – the wins had kept us four points behind the leaders but a defeat and two scoreless draws knocked us back to seven adrift. A home draw with Middlesbrough didn't help matters but we were able to find some form when we came up against Brighton & Hove Albion – I was particularly pleased with my own performance that day. I'd found some comfort and confidence in my midfield role and I was spraying balls about the pitch, out wide to the wingers, I was having a game where everything went well. My team-mates all played well, too, and we were in a strong position of 3-1 late in the game thanks to a couple of goals from Joe Jordan.

Ashley Grimes had come on as a substitute and darted into the box to make a run – I shouted to him, 'Over', which meant for him to leave the ball and let it go through his legs as I was on the edge of the six-yard box. He did just that and I hit it with my left foot – it was blocked by a combination of the goalkeeper and defender, but rebounded straight to me and I tucked it in with my right foot from a couple of yards out. I didn't know what to do! Celebrating other people's goals is one thing but I just really didn't know what to do, it was manic – and it topped off a great win and performance for us. It showed how much it meant to me; the goal didn't influence the result but just to score my first goal in the First Division was unreal.

I wasn't to know but that started a connection with Brighton between myself and the club that was to last about 19 months; I suppose it's a bit of an odd club to have that with but football is full of coincidences like that and things that appear to be fated or would seem contrived if they'd been written. Managers who get sacked, take over a new club and immediately face their old one, players who do the same after a transfer and then score. It happens so often and for me Brighton would become a club I'd be familiar with over the next couple of years.

Draws, as I've said, can be a good result for momentum but as that middle-of-the-road result they can also have the opposite effect and seem like a result that isn't so great. Following the victory over Brighton we didn't win in six games, with two defeats making the four draws look like points dropped – even with what would normally seem like a decent result in a 0-0 against Liverpool on Boxing Day – but at the turn of the year we remained seven points behind the pace that was being set by Liverpool. That draw with the leaders was our 15th in 24 games – they themselves had drawn 12 – but they'd also won 11 games to our six. We were unbeaten at home but had drawn nine of our 12 games at Old Trafford and that was proving to be the major problem as we attempted to contend for the title.

With Garry Birtles failing to set the world alight and the workmanlike performances of the likes of Mickey Thomas and Joe Jordan as opposed to the flashier displays from Tommy Doc's side, Dave Sexton was for the first time finding it difficult and drawing criticism from supporters who were not enjoying the style of play. Dave was a thoughtful man, very studious, and I felt he was criticised a little unfairly for being negative.

He would always encourage me to attack; when I played at full-back, he would say as soon as Stevie Coppell got the ball, I should just bomb past him. Asking a full-back to overlap and not just support – how is that negative? From the supporters' point of view, though, I could see where they were coming from even if just in the personnel and the make-up of some of the players Dave had brought in. 'Workhorse' seems like a slight, a criticism, but nobody can make it at United without putting in their best and Dave wanted to make sure that was a quality of anyone he brought in.

After United had come back up and won the FA Cup, and then finished second, supporters were expecting some kind of real progression and what they were seeing in the performances and results was not to their liking. The supporters have a right to voice their opinion and even though I felt I was doing well maybe my own role in that could have been seen as negative; I was a sensible midfield player and like I said I felt I was playing well, but as I could later be described as an attacking full-back, it would have been generous to have described me as an attacking midfield player.

Margins in football at the highest level can be very small and it could simply be that gamble on Garry Birtles going wrong when it could, and perhaps should, have easily gone right and been the deciding factor in us winning the title. If anyone had asked me at the time, 'Is Garry Birtles a player you want to sign?' I would definitely have said yes. But it just didn't happen for him (coincidentally, a similar pattern would follow later with the signing of Alan Brazil which I also thought was great at the time) and it wasn't going right for Dave either. Garry would come good in his second season and enjoyed some decent form but the stigma that had come with going so long without a goal had already affected his reputation, so much so that there was that joke doing the rounds about Terry Waite, claiming that when he'd been released from his hostage ordeal his first question was, 'Has Garry Birtles scored for United yet?'

Aside from Garry's first game at Stoke, where I'd come on as substitute, I'd found myself as a regular first-teamer from the start in midfield but I was back on the bench for the FA Cup third round tie against Brighton. One or two of their lads said to me, 'I can't believe you're not playing, when we saw the teamsheet and you were on the bench we were so relieved.' It was great, and a fantastic confidence boost to keep my spirits up after being named as a sub. As the game wore on and United were struggling, one or two pockets around Old Trafford had begun to boo and show discontent.

I came on for Sammy McIlroy to the most wonderful ovation – I'm really not one to blow my own trumpet, so to speak, though including all the praise that was said to me perhaps makes me look like I protest too much! – though as invigorating as it was to receive such a warm welcome from the supporters I'd once stood among, I couldn't help but feel sorry for Sammy, who'd been an incredible servant to the club. He was coming towards the end but still had great ability; I'd like to think that the cheers were just for me and not for Sammy going off. Personally, I was on a rush with the adrenalin and with my first touch, as the ball was cleared to me from a defensive corner, I raced up the length of the pitch and attempted to whip the ball in – it was cleared for a corner for us, which Mickey Thomas scored from. That brought us back to 2-1, and I was delighted when I was able to score myself to rescue a draw and earn us a replay.

Despite my contribution, I was again named as substitute for the replay. For the first time, I was approached by press asking if I was unhappy, and asking why I wasn't playing. I knew what they were angling for, but I just told them that the manager picks his team and it was his decision. It would have been easy to say I didn't know and that I felt he should have picked me, but I wasn't one to rock the boat. Privately, of course, I was very disappointed.

To come on and influence a positive result and have that momentum of having given the crowd a lift you naturally feel that such a boost will play in your favour. Dave wasn't the type to tell you why you'd been dropped and so I had that to contend with, too. If I'd felt more authoritative maybe I would have gone and asked myself, but I didn't, and I couldn't accuse Dave of hypocrisy because it wasn't as if I'd been given an explanation of why I'd been selected in the first place. I came on as sub in the replay, which we won – and in a case of deja vu, the next game was also against Brighton, this time in the league, and I was substitute in a win. I missed the fourth round tie with Nottingham Forest, which saw us eliminated, but would find myself back in the team afterwards.

By now – with cup exits, below-par performances and even finding his selections questioned publicly by the press – the pressure was really on Dave to succeed but defeat at Sunderland in the game I was recalled certainly didn't help. Entering February, we were in ninth place, nine points behind Ipswich at the top and out of both cups. Dave's persona was such that you would never see if the pressure was getting to him; he had his moments where he could snap or have a go if something wasn't right and I certainly wouldn't have liked to have gotten in the way of that. He must have felt the pressure internally but he didn't let it show externally. He stuck with things, for better or worse, showing conviction in his opinion.

Defeat to Leicester – who were second-bottom – put us 11 points behind Ipswich which really heightened the tension for Dave, and also spelled the end of Nicola Jovanovic's Manchester United career. Nikki was the first foreign-signed player at the club (discounting the academy product Carlo Sartori in the 1970s) and I just think he never really settled. He was a lovely man – a skilful, strong player with two good feet – but I think he just didn't settle. As one on his own, it was always going to be difficult moving and trying to acclimatise.

I can't say for sure as I simply don't know what went on with the more senior players, whether they offered to try and help. Knowing what a good bunch they were, they may well have done. He was okay language-wise, but without the same kind of integration that is so prolific in today's game maybe it's fair to say that the odds were stacked against him. Injury problems didn't help and I don't think Tommy Cav was overly sympathetic towards his situation either – unfamiliar with how tough England could be, perhaps it's fair to say that wasn't the best or happiest time for Nikki. He couldn't have had much help due to his situation and I was sorry to him go.

Home draws with Spurs and Forest sandwiched a defeat in the derby at Maine Road and those three results, following the loss at Filbert Street, put us well and truly out of the title picture, if we were ever seriously in it. Yet to prove what a funny game football can be, as soon as the pressure of expectancy was off, we started to blossom. A run of wins started with victory over league leaders Ipswich who had only suffered two losses all season; we then got a great win at Everton, before facing Crystal Palace at home. I was the sole goalscorer in a 1-0 win – Mick Duxbury, Manchester United match-winner, though funnily enough I didn't celebrate half as crazily as I did when I scored my first against Brighton.

I remember the goal clearly; I was just jogging up to support, and Joe Jordan had the ball on the left-hand side. Palace were a great side and had some fantastic young players – Dario Gradi was continuing some wonderful work done by Terry Venables there. One of their top players was a lad called Vince Hilaire who should have been tracking me and later confided in me that he thought I was going to take a couple of touches to set it up and then he'd have plenty of time to get a tackle in. Joe played the ball into me and I hit it first time as it sat up just right – I've seen photographs of it since, and I remember people always saying, 'Imagine there's a photographer and you're posing' – this pose seemed almost picture perfect! I caught it great and it went just inside the post. It must have been a good assist – most of the players went over to Joe to celebrate, and I wondered what was going on!

After the defeat to City you might have thought it was understandable if the manager had been sacked after the pressure he was under, but then to enjoy the run of games and wins that we had – we closed the season with seven consecutive victories – seemed to be a big shock. Especially as those wins began with the two points against Ipswich and also included a success at Anfield. It's always special to go up there and get a good result, and for whatever reason we always seemed to. It was a tense atmosphere; Gordon McQueen gave us the lead, and I remember defending the Kop end in the last few minutes, scrambling the ball away to see the game out. It was a great atmosphere to play in, which as always our great travelling fans contributed towards, and I can't remember getting any abuse that was too bad.

By this point I'd started to play at right-back, and I must confess that I felt a little bit embarrassed to be taking the position of Jimmy Nicholl at the time. Jimmy had been through the system that I had and he'd been there for a long time; maybe he wasn't playing at his absolute best. I was glad to have a role in the side but I was sad for Jimmy too. Playing down the touchline brings you closer to the fans though by this time I'd learned to block the atmosphere out enough to fully concentrate on the game. It might have helped that my early games were through the middle in that respect.

Our fixture list concluded on 25 April with a win at Old Trafford over Norwich City. We finished in eighth position, with nine losses. Aston Villa, the eventual champions, had only lost eight, which showed the damage that those draws ultimately did for us. Eighteen draws absolutely cost us; it was a horrible irony that we'd seemed to have found a way to see out the close games and get wins by the time it was too late for Dave Sexton.

I was actually at Old Trafford when the news broke that he'd been sacked – I was milling about in the players' lounge. If there was a feeling that I had, then 'stunned' sums it up. It had been such an optimistic end to the season – seven wins, and nine games unbeaten. At the time, I wasn't one for establishing a lot of contact with my team-mates and colleagues outside of the club and away from football, so that was essentially the last of my contact with Dave as United manager. I would go on to work with him again, though with hindsight maybe I should have called or written to him in the immediate aftermath of his departure.

I could see both sides of it and with the way football is there could certainly be no complaints that Dave had lost his job simply because of the expectation levels at Manchester United but I was very disappointed and sad to see him go – I'd have perhaps given him the start of the next season, to see if he'd managed to get past his rough spell, but you could see the sense in making a break so a new man could come in with a full pre-season to get settled.

Personally, after so long trying to establish myself, as the season came to a close I was finally feeling I had done that, and with Dave's departure, that nagging doubt I had that I was going to have to prove myself all over again for a new manager surfaced. I wasn't alone; we were all in the same position in having to prove ourselves to the next person to take the manager's job. I wasn't exactly back to square one but not so far away from that; if there's one thing that you could conclude from the exit of Dave Sexton as United manager, it's that there was very much an air of uncertainty at Old Trafford.

5

'Whatever you are,
be a good one.'

Anon

I DON'T know whether it would be right to say just being English and playing for Manchester United is enough to earn you a call-up these days and it would probably be unfair for me to make such a judgement. The numbers suggest that is the case, though the argument would probably be turned around – if you're good enough to play for Manchester United, you're probably good enough to be selected for England.

There are exceptions of course but in 1981, with England's top flight predominantly filled with British players, playing the national team represented the natural pinnacle when looking at the ascent.

I'd like to think that it was my ability and not the fact that my manager at Manchester United at the time, Dave Sexton, gave me my first call-up to the under-21s in November 1980. Certainly, no-one could accuse him of club bias as I was the only United player. It was a good team that were involved in the European Championship qualifying campaign, with the likes of Chris Woods in goal, Alan Curbishley, Lee Chapman,

Steve McMahon, Remi Moses and Vince Hilaire, whom I discussed in the last chapter. Qualifiers against Switzerland and Romania at Portman Road and Swindon's County Ground respectively saw comprehensive victories while we also got a win over Ireland at Anfield in February 1981.

The game against Romania was a strange one as it came just a day or two after Dave had been let go against United. I can't recall any interaction with him, even to pass on my sympathy. As I've said before, maybe looking back at it I should have done. He was still a manager of mine so it didn't feel too strange to be playing under him. As we were due to head abroad to play a qualifier and a friendly, Howard Wilkinson, who was the England C manager, took charge. As the under-21s went to Switzerland we were still not entirely sure who would be the next United manager. We got a good draw against the Swiss in a game that was uneventful and for the best, considering some hooligan trouble that had gone on between the senior side's loss in Basel the day before. Uneventful, that is, aside from an ankle injury to myself that ruled me out of the friendly win against Hungary a few days later.

It was clear that all was not settled at Old Trafford; I had been part of the team that flew out to Tel Aviv for a friendly in early May where we got to see Jerusalem. Long-haul travels for one-off friendly fixtures seemed like a bit of a pain but were part and parcel of the way the game was heading and it seemed that we would take more out of it from a tourist perspective rather than a sporting one.

Being with England, I had missed the first leg of United's post-season trip to the Far East but I was hearing plenty about things that weren't quite right at home. I don't think I was originally required to go on the trip but I received word that I must go as players were dropping out. I flew direct from Hungary to Malaysia. By this point, it was pretty much decided that Ron Atkinson was the man to succeed Dave in the United hotseat but Jack Crompton, the long-serving trainer, looked after us while we were away. Another interim coach, but one I knew a lot more than Howard Wilkinson.

Jack was such a gentleman, really nice – he was a familiar face around United, having played for such a long time and being there as a trainer too. If we went back for afternoon training to do weights or circuits, it would always be Jack there to take us. If there was one thing you could say about Jack, it would be that he was simply too nice to ever really be manager of Manchester United, particularly if it came to older professionals and egos. And that's not a bad thing – Jack was a fantastic man and I, like many others, was so very sad when he passed away in 2013.

It was a tour that nobody really wanted to be on, if I'm being honest. It was okay, I guess, but with everything going on it just seemed a massive inconvenience – it was my first real long trip away as a first-teamer and I arrived just in time to play against an invitational side in Sabah. The heat and humidity was unbelievable – we were having chunks of ice thrown on to us on the pitch to cool us down but it was barely helping. The facilities weren't great and neither were the hotels we were staying at. For a few reasons, it wasn't the most exciting or memorable (at least for the right reasons) but ultimately you're representing United, there's protocol to follow and a professional way to behave.

My own late inclusion on the trip was due to the suggested unprofessional behaviour of others who had missed it. I was in the dark – it wasn't until I caught up with the rest of the squad that I would know what had actually happened, and even then you're relying on second-hand news so it's not always easy to form an opinion. Three players didn't come with us out to Malaysia and those were Sammy McIlroy, Jimmy Nicholl and Mickey Thomas. In Sammy and Jimmy's case, both had played for Northern Ireland and were feeling the strain of the travel

– and Sammy's son was ill, so it was understandable that he didn't come out. Mickey Thomas's absence is a lot easier to discuss because he himself tells the story! My take on it was that Sammy and Jimmy had already left before Mickey did; and I think Mickey actually changed his mind right at the last minute.

On the surface, Mickey is a very affable and bubbly person but underneath that exterior he had a lot of insecurities and was struggling to deal with playing for Manchester United. I roomed with him quite often and I don't know what it was but he could never keep still, he couldn't relax. After dinner in the hotels, some of the lads would stay down in the bar or lobby for a bit longer but I'd go back up into the room and watch a bit of television. Mickey just couldn't settle and was always on edge, he always had to be doing something, and I suppose you could see similarities in the way that he played too, jerky and jittery, something that was in his make-up. You could argue that he was always going to struggle as soon as he signed – his arrival was very much a symbolic one, one that would appear to be emblematic of Dave Sexton's reign.

Mickey was a solid, hard-working player but replaced Gordon Hill – it was an unpopular sale at the time and though Mickey himself was never unpopular with fans, he struggled to live up to the expectations of flamboyance and that seemed to weigh him down. To be perfectly honest, though, Mickey wasn't the only player dealing with being known as a 'Sexton' player as opposed to a 'Docherty' player. You can have your own views on how well Dave did, but there is little doubt that giving someone the 'Sexton' tag is not really a complimentary one by comparison to the latter. Some handled it better; Joe Jordan and Gordon McQueen were robust enough to deal with it.

I can only speculate and perhaps it's not fair to do so but with Sexton's style proving so unpopular with supporters, it could be that Mickey took it personally too, and when Dave left, those insecurities simply got the better of him. He was a lovely lad, though, I must stress that! As someone who wasn't naturally extroverted I sympathised with Mickey and maybe I benefitted from the simple fact I'd come through the youth system. As an outsider, for want of a better phrase, for whatever reason, some struggle to cope with the size and enormity of playing for the club. Is it on the field, are there outside influences? There's a lot to put together and however you analyse it, the end result for Mickey was that it was too much for him.

The same could be said for Garry Birtles – and let's remember, again, that at the time of their signings they appeared to be decent additions that nobody would have necessarily said no to at the time.

For me, the idea is almost alien – players arriving at Old Trafford come with the notion that everyone is a superstar there and that's the role they have to live up to yet for me that couldn't be further from the truth. I suffered from nerves at times but never to the extent that Mickey – visibly – and Garry, I'm sure internally, would feel. I was more comfortable than them and so you wonder if perhaps you could have done more to help; you do what you can on the pitch but once they go home they are their own people.

Everyone has to handle it in their own way. I'd always done things in my own way and at my own pace and I was afforded that – I was never under any pressure from the manager or squad to change the way I was. Like I say, at the time when I was younger I felt I was stagnating but now, as one of the quiet younger players on the squad, it felt more natural. I was allowed to be that way but maybe as a player coming in, particularly into a position where there have been so many great personalities in the past, you simply cannot appreciate just how great the pressure is to live up to it.

In the summer of 1981 it wasn't a case of one or two Sexton players sticking out like sore thumbs; it was very much a squad that Dave had put together, with Ray Wilkins having signed and Jimmy Greenhoff and Andy Ritchie leaving Old Trafford the previous season. You could even say that I was more of a Dave Sexton style player, most definitely you could have said that I was more that than a Tommy Docherty style. As with Dave's team, there were a couple of players who truly summed up The Doc's team. Gordon Hill had been one and he was sold on fairly quickly, Brian Greenhoff was another, a midfielder who'd moved back into centre-half but who very clearly concentrated on attacking. He signed for Leeds in 1979 – like Jack Crompton, I was saddened to hear of his death in 2013. He'd always been good to me and shortly before he passed on he sent me a copy of his own autobiography congratulating me on my own career – that was Brian, a class act who had gone out of his way to make sure I got a picture with the FA Cup in 1977.

And I think that's what I mean about the difference in character or at least perception of character of those at Old Trafford; for those on the outside coming in, they see the glamour and the glory, and those who work from the inside know how hard we have to work to make the grade and appreciate that. That's not to say that those coming in don't appreciate it, just that perhaps some who do come in do not immediately understand just how hard everyone at the club is expected to work.

I certainly knew! And I was more of a Sexton-type player, I'd grown accustomed to his training methods and the way that he'd encouraged me had a profound impact on my game. As I'd converted to full-back pretty late in the 1980/81 season, if I'd just been allowed to hide in my shell to an extent, I may not have lasted very long, but Dave encouraged me to go forward and overlap Stevie Coppell. It'll be the final thing I say about it, but I do feel Dave perhaps suffered in that no matter how attacking he tried to be, it was always going to be not quite as gung-ho as Tommy Docherty before him. No two managers are the same; Dave was a student of the game who would have us watching videos of great players.

He showed me videos of Beckenbauer, and of course everyone knows that he was a great player, but it was only on closely observing him in the manner Dave wanted you to that you could truly appreciate how outstanding he was. He would encourage you to adopt the same kind of mannerisms, making you watch the footage to understand how Franz had that great sense of anticipation and timing. The right kind of footage of the right player at the right time can do wonders for your own game if you take the right kind of messages on board; as a young player sometimes your concentration can wander and you'll be wanting to just get out and play! Looking back, I have a greater appreciation for what Dave was doing and I only wish I could have watched one of those tapes on Bobby Moore. What an inspirational player he was. At the time, though, you're more obstinate and more concentrating on your own game, not necessarily wanting to learn from other people.

The appointment of Ron Atkinson was made official by the time I'd landed in Malaysia. He'd a good reputation and had done well with West Brom, with Bryan Robson and Laurie Cunningham. I felt it was a good appointment and just as Dave Sexton represented a huge personality shift from his predecessor, it was exactly the same with Ron. He came with a reputation of being flashy and instead of trying to move away from it or dispel it, he seemed only to live up to it and try and grow into it even more. He couldn't have been any more different to Dave.

I wasn't exactly fearful for my future but as someone with just one season in senior football under my belt, you naturally have a concern about where you will figure in the new manager's plans. Dave himself had been no stranger to making huge and unexpected changes so you have to prepare yourself for anything. I could not argue to be an established member of the team just yet, in any case. I knew that from day one I'd be battling to prove myself; within reason, my form in 1980/81 would count for little as we returned for pre-season training.

There were big changes immediately; whereas Dave had kept Tommy Cavanagh on, Ron made sweeping alterations by bringing his own staff in, Mick Brown as his assistant and Brian Whiteside as a first-team coach. There was a big turnaround; fresh faces replacing those that we'd known for a long time. It was a new start, a new challenge and it wasn't always comfortable in the early days getting used to the change in methods. With the absence of Tommy Cav, there wasn't even a familiar face to go to and sound off about any niggling concerns we had. Just a few days into the pre-season, our new physio Jim Headridge was jogging around The Cliff with some of the young lads when he suddenly collapsed and died right in front of the goalmouth. It was absolutely tragic and a shock to us all. Jim McGregor was then brought in as the new physio – everything seemed like such a huge upheaval that it was surreal, almost to the extent that it felt like a different club.

With training barely back under way, Ron made moves which justified my own concerns when he decided to bring in John Gidman, a right-sided defender, from Everton. It certainly didn't feel brilliant. Mickey Thomas's future at United was always going to be in question after he got off the plane that was headed to Malaysia and he was used as the collateral in John's transfer. Mickey wasn't the only player leaving, though – Joe Jordan moved to Italian giants AC Milan.

The pre-season fixtures only seemed to exacerbate my worries as John was selected more often than not and I found myself either out of position or as a substitute, but I knew that even in midfield, my chances were likely to be limited as Ron was making very public moves to sign Bryan Robson. I'd got to the point where I was reasoning with myself that because Bryan was left-footed, I could be used as a perfect foil beside him. There was no getting away from the fact that it was going to be very tough for me to establish myself.

Unsurprisingly, I started the season in the reserves. A year prior, I'd had the fleeting thought that I might have to go away, even if only on loan, to get some football, but it was much too early to give up on my dream of playing for United now I'd been given a taste of it. Besides, at the point I was at, what good would a loan move have done me anyway? Loans are basically there to get you experience as a youngster and I wasn't going to break into the first team and prove my worth if I was somewhere else. If there was one thing I had achieved in my short career to that point, it was proving myself worthy of that chance and taking it when I got there and it was just the way that football goes that I was in that position again a year later. I wouldn't call it a setback or even a stagnation but it was frustrating to say the least. You begin to wonder what it will take to get back in, if it was going to be as much down to luck or misfortune on someone else's part as it would be my own form.

It wasn't an easy start for Ron – his first game was a 2-1 defeat at Coventry in which John Gidman played at right-back with Ray Wilkins and Lou Macari in midfield. Up front we had another new signing, Frank Stapleton, who had often been the scourge of United in the past. Frank had true pedigree for Arsenal, he almost represented a sure bet with his history of playing for such a top club. Of course, it helped that his wife Christine was a Manchester girl and he was able to settle in very quickly. He proved to be a very good player for the club, an excellent signing. Another player coming in was a midfielder from West Brom who Ron Atkinson knew well, but not Bryan Robson just yet – Remi Moses was someone I'd known from England under-21 duty and I thought he was a great signing for us. Again, though, it was competition for myself! Remi was a midfielder but could easily have played at full-back too.

The new faces were proving to be extra competition but, in a strange way, also helped me feel like more of an established member of the squad. Allow me to explain. Being on the edge of Tommy Docherty's squad wasn't exactly like being an outsider but there was very much an established group of senior players, a squad that remained together for a while. The influx of players and change around under Dave benefitted me in my rise into the team and while I initially found it difficult at some points to feel settled, once Ron had started to bring in three or four new players, they were all eager to integrate and it was almost as if we were all doing that together. I suppose it's a difficult thing to rationalise.

Squad turnover and changes may well have been the defining factor in the unsettled start to the season which continued with a draw against Forest and then a home defeat to Ipswich in which Frank scored his first goal for the club; I came on as a substitute in that game for my first appearance of the season. Though I would not have levelled club bias at Dave Sexton for selecting me for the under-21s before, maybe it stood in my favour that he was familiar with me as a player as I was called up for my fifth under-21 cap against Norway in a friendly in September 1981. Having just turned 22, I was eligible for the European Championships which were due to take place over the coming season due to the fact I'd been young enough to be included when the competition began.

I was under no illusions though that to retain my place, I'd have to make sure I was getting into the United team. It was a little difficult to take – you understand that a new manager comes in and has his own ideas but again, I felt I'd done well enough to at least deserve the chance to show what I could do and I was concerned I wasn't getting enough game time in the early weeks of the campaign. After the international break, I once again came on as substitute, this time at Middlesbrough in a 2-0 win. Garry Birtles had finally scored his first league goal for the club in the previous game against Swansea and scored at Ayresome Park – positively prolific at this point!

I was seeing sporadic opportunities as a sub and when I got my first chance to start, in the return fixture against Middlesbrough in mid-October, I felt I played really well, hitting the bar with an effort from about 30 yards. It was a game we won. I was in midfield, though I was probably looking to right-back or in defence, at least, as my long-term role in the team. I don't know if it's a matter of professional pride or just human nature but you look at the ability of those who are in your position and wonder if they're better than you.

I don't want to pull Giddy down but if Bryan Robson, a world-class player, is stopping you getting a game then you know the reason why and can openly accept it. I didn't think John was better than me and I didn't think his form at the time was any better than I'd shown the previous year so in that respect it was ultimately down to the manager and his preference. When looking at it like that, you then start to question the judgement of the manager. Though, as someone directly affected by his choices in a negative way, then maybe it's expected that I would be questioning it. It was too early for me to form a properly negative opinion about Ron, but it's safe to say that we didn't get off to the best of starts.

For better or worse, having signed John, he was probably under pressure to select him from the start anyway and he may have been open to questions if he hadn't. That's the external view which is simplistic and doesn't give you the insight of what happens inside the club and I have to be honest and say that I didn't feel that Giddy was the best trainer; I wouldn't say he feigned stuff, but he'd take it easy and appear to pull the wool over people's eyes. I thought I was doing everything right, and I honestly couldn't see why he was being selected in front of me. I was behaving in a professional manner and taking everything much more seriously than it appeared John was, so particularly after I'd worked so hard to get that opportunity, it was difficult to handle in those early weeks.

People have been critical of Dave Sexton's personality but he was, to me, at least someone I could talk to. Ron was brash, larger than life – or at least wanted dearly to put that impression across – and sometimes in training it appeared as if he'd set up the session purely to satisfy his own ego. He'd join in – which was fine, managers did that – but there were certain drills with crossing, finishing, and he'd be in those too. Who was the one who was supposed to be benefitting? The full-backs putting in the crosses, the forwards trying to finish them, or the manager who was just having fun? As a youngster who didn't have that kind of personality, I just observed it and felt he wasn't the kind of person I could approach seriously with concerns.

That's not to say that I felt Ron didn't take the opportunity seriously, I'm sure he did, and his preparation for matches was good enough to show you that. There were just instances like the one above, or even unplanned pre-season training. We went to Heaton Park, which was a regular occurrence with United, and it was always well planned. However on this particular day, we went to do some running and when we arrived there was a woman with a pram – he was just telling us to run around the woman! Thoughts then occurred, what happened if she wasn't there, or even if she moved as we were running? There was no respect for how she'd feel with 30 blokes bombing towards her, and I don't think she'd be on the pitch on the Saturday either!

John Gidman was no Bryan Robson, but the real thing himself arrived at Manchester United in early October of 1981. He was the real deal who was going to leave nobody in any illusions about how seriously he would take playing for the club. The signing gave a real lift to everyone at the club, except perhaps for Sammy McIlroy. On the day Bryan signed, Sammy scored a hat-trick against Wolverhampton Wanderers, but it was overshadowed not only by the new arrival but by the fact there was mounting speculation that Robbo was there to take his place.

Personally, I felt it was a great statement of intent from Sammy and I even said to Robbo afterwards that it was that kind of performance that was expected from him at United. But Bryan, like Frank, was almost nailed on to be a success at Manchester United. Sammy had done so many great things at United – he was a Busby Babe who'd been playing at the club since he was 17 and at 27, was just about at what should have been his peak. He'd seen many great players come and go so there wasn't really a question about whether he could play with Bryan, but it was more a case of what the signing of Robson meant with regards the manager's own opinion of him. It seemed clear that Ron would prefer Robson to McIlroy and it seemed just as clear, in training at least, that Ron and Sammy didn't exactly see eye to eye.

Five years older than me, perhaps Sammy couldn't afford to take the chance and wait as I had, and unfortunately that meant that he was going to be gone sooner rather than later. Every player knows that the end of his time will come; he had his testimonial in the November of 1981 which I unfortunately didn't play in, but soon after that he was transferred to Stoke City. Personally, I didn't have a connection with some of the older players in the squad like, perhaps, Sammy, and it's always said that a manager is the most important person at the club.

When a manager has just come in, he can afford to make one or two bold choices even if they are unpopular. I was personally very disappointed when he left because I felt he had so much to offer; it's been said that you can't have sentiment in football and that was how Ron must have looked at it. It will be something I will explain later, but being brutally honest I had reservations about Ron right from the start and his decision to sell Sammy strengthened those feelings of concern.

I was seeing the odd sniff of first-team football but after starting in the defeat to Spurs, it would be a couple of months until I was back in the side again, though that had a lot to do with the weather. There was a 'big freeze' that saw United without a competitive game for almost a month; when I was back in the fold against Stoke City we won to go third, two points behind Ipswich, though we'd played twice more than them. The league form compensated for the poor form in the cups – we'd suffered two early exits, to Tottenham in the League Cup and Watford in the third round of the FA Cup, and maybe it was that which saw me recalled on a more regular basis.

I hadn't been given a reason for why I was put back in the team – and, to give Ron his dues, that was okay for me. It was the same with Dave, he didn't tell me why he selected me so didn't tell me why he'd drop or rest me; as long as there was consistency in that, even though I might be disappointed, it wasn't as if I could throw the toys out of the pram. Now I was back in the team, getting that chance, it was up to me to make sure I kept it. I got back in at right-back but John returned to the team and I found myself in midfield alongside Bryan.

There was no opportunity to rest on my laurels and see how things went. I knew now how fierce the competition was and it was up to me to make sure I made a statement, and I knew it wasn't always going to be easy. I was at number ten in midfield in the game against Aston Villa on 6 February 1982 and I was the youngest player in the starting line-up, at the age of 22. My inclusion in the team had shown that my competition for a starting place wouldn't only be John Gidman, it would be anyone in the squad, so there was no chance of hanging about, I had to show everyone what I was made of.

A win at Wolves – with Birtles the lone goalscorer – moved us into a great position where we were two points behind the leaders Southampton with a game in hand. That was my 50th appearance for the United first team and looking around the squad there was a mixture of players like Martin Buchan, Arthur Albiston and Steve Coppell who were vastly experienced and then a handful of players like myself, Kevin Moran and Ray Wilkins who'd had just about a season and a half of playing in the first team as well as the new arrivals.

Ron had got the reputation of a more flamboyant character than Dave Sexton but the football wasn't profoundly different to me; playing alongside Bryan Robson as I was doing, I was the holding or more disciplined of the two while Bryan would be the all-action player we knew and loved. There was a structure and a discipline that we all understood, I don't think it would be worth giving Ron any undue credit for being cavalier in comparison to Dave.

There had been a huge change in football in the 1981/82 season and that was that clubs were awarded three points for a win instead of two. It had a big impact on many teams but as far as Manchester United were concerned the expectancy was to win, so nothing would ever change in that regard. I played almost 400 times for the club and every single time we went out to win, there were no exceptions. Looking at the shape of the league at the turn of the year and the away form of teams in the bottom half, you might say that there had been a shift in mentality where teams felt their home form would be good enough to compensate for their away form; for example, Leeds enjoyed a long run where they were unbeaten at home but lost almost every game on the road. That didn't help them, as they lay in 18th position, but it was a familiar pattern throughout the league with teams trying to make their home a fortress. Just as there'd been no change in emphasis from our point of view anyway, we knew just what to expect from the opposition and that never changed either.

Ironically, given the way things would turn out, I think when Sir Alex Ferguson came and took over at United, he was the manager who would concentrate more on the opposition than any other boss I'd worked under at the club. At the time, under Ron, it was very much a feeling of concentrating on our own strengths.

There was a very strong sense of belief around the squad that we could win the league as we went into March. After beating Birmingham, we were four points behind Southampton with two games in hand and had lost fewer games than anyone in the First Division. Eight matches later we were above Southampton on goal difference with a game in hand – unfortunately for us, that was only because they'd suffered even worse form than we had. We'd only won in three of those eight games – and I'd only played in the games we didn't win – as Liverpool stole a march with a run of wins to put them top. Losing at home to them, and then at Ipswich, were the killer results for us. Ten points behind with six games left, the league was realistically up for us and we managed to finish in decent form, winning five and drawing one of those games, putting us in a final position of third.

Ending the season optimistically after such a turbulent start could only be seen as a positive and it was equally uplifting when Norman Whiteside, the young Irish forward, came into the side towards the end of the season and performed so well.

He was like a man when he came into the squad as a 16-year-old – I often would say he was ten when he was born! Norman was a superb player, the most natural finisher at the club. He came in and played up front; he had tremendous aggression and a wonderful left foot, giving the whole club a boost. If you're 16 and playing in the United first team it's obvious that you're special, not just a run-of-the-mill player, and it was always on the cards for Norman. Physically he could more than cope, mentally, he was ready – whereas for me it might have killed me! It showed how incredibly well he'd settled in that he was immediately called up for Northern Ireland and was taken to the 1982 World Cup.

Expectations and hopes are always high when a new manager takes over and while we might have expected to do a bit better in the cup competitions, to finish third in the league was definitely a start that could be described as 'okay' to say the least. Looking back on it, with us finishing seven points ahead of Tottenham who were in fourth place, having us well established as the third best team in the league was probably a fair reflection of where we were at the time. It wasn't a God-given right for us to be up at the top but it felt like our purpose to be challenging for the league and we were on the right steps.

Players like Robson and Whiteside who had come in to the team and given us big boosts had made us believe that we could achieve more. The late season dip in form was disappointing but made us all that more determined to right those wrongs the following year. One player who wouldn't be with us to see if we could make that step would be Garry Birtles. His second season had been much better but just not enough; he'd settled in a lot better than Mickey Thomas did off the pitch but couldn't quite get it going in games.

For me, after a very disappointing start, the run of games at the end saw me finish with 25 appearances for the season which I saw as a big achievement. I'd finished on a high, and just as with the end of my first year in the first team, I was so optimistic looking forward. This time, having battled my way back, I was able to reflect and view myself as a member of the squad. I still had the nagging doubt that I would ever be Ron's first choice – that would always remain – yet with the change in personnel I definitely felt like I was part of the squad, growing up with them.

Whereas in 1980/81 I'd made my mark as a right-back in the end, now I was a midfielder contending with the likes of Bryan Robson and Remi Moses – the only thing certain about the immediate future was that I'd fought my way into contention, and that was reason enough to look forward to the next campaign.

6

Que Sera Sera

FOR a long time following the 1980s, once the season was over players went on their holidays until their pre-season began. It wasn't uncommon for clubs to have money-spinning trips abroad at the end of a long season; though I'd been on the one the previous year after joining the squad in Malaysia from the under-21s, the trip to Vancouver at the end of the 1981/82 season was the first I'd taken complete part in.

Our long trips didn't always end up with us playing competitive games but we were in Canada to play the Europac Tournament – I played in all the matches and was presented with the award for the best player. It was the first time I'd been that way and it was a beautiful place; it was in that tournament when I first came up against Peter Beardsley. Truth be told, I remember very little of coming up against him in the tournament as I didn't play against him directly but I do recall there being talk of how impressed people were after the game. It must have been that impression that convinced Ron to bring him to Old Trafford for a couple of months afterwards. I scored in the final game, against Hajduk Split on an astroturf pitch. Following the boom in interest in the game in the 1970s with the likes of Pele, Beckenbauer and Best, the early 1980s were a little bit of an interim period for football in North America and Canada. There were reports of financial struggles over there and so we weren't surprised to play in front of relatively small crowds of around 13,000.

There was no time to stay and enjoy a holiday in Canada; I returned with the squad back to the UK to prepare for my wedding to Karen on 26 June 1982. We'd lived for about a year previous to getting married, in a house in Helmshore, Rossendale. We were married at our local church which Karen had lived 50 yards down the road from, and enjoyed a nice quiet honeymoon shortly after. We went up to the Lakes and a little bit later there was a supporters' club do in Malta, so we enjoyed a few days out there too. It was a good time – following what had been a difficult start to the previous season, it had ended in the right way and everything seemed to be rolling the right way.

We tended to report back for pre-season on the same day, around 18 or 19 July. Part of our preparation in the summer of 1982 was a trip to Iceland which was made really memorable by the inclusion of George Best. He travelled on the plane out with us and it was absolutely brilliant; he was among the team and I remember speaking to him on the plane. He was sat next to me at one point – I'd been drifting off to sleep and then all of a sudden someone woke me up to ask for an autograph. George said to me, 'Nice to see they leave you alone,' but I don't think he meant anything sarcastic by it! He must have had that hundreds of times worse than me!

He was with us in the hotel but sadly wasn't going to be on our side, he was to line up with the opposition. By this stage George was really struggling with his knees so was a shadow of his former self and if I'm brutally honest then it was a bit disappointing. It would have been nice to see him and play with him in his prime. Or maybe not, considering he was on the opposition side – that would have been hard work! He was still capable of magic but it was rare; even to have seen him at the level he was renowned for playing at in America would have been nice.

On a personal level, I thought George was a great person. I would only go on to meet him two or three times in my career but I felt he was a really nice guy – someone like George carried that 'Manchester United superstar' aura about them and it always remained. He was someone you looked up to, and he wasn't the only one – Bobby Charlton, Denis Law, Nobby Stiles, players who had achieved greatness but as people they always went out of their way to put us at ease. We had a more than capable squad with some big names in our own right and I myself had played more than 50 times for United so could be described as having had some experience but I still felt star-struck around the likes of George and Bobby. It eased over time yet an element of it always remained; as I became more established, I would become more recognised by these greats, but a part of you still retains that starry-eyed feeling. That was due to what they had accomplished and been in the game rather than anything they'd act up towards – George would always speak to you, he never acted like he was above you, and the same went for Bobby or Sir Matt, I always felt that if you were walking down the street and bumped into them they'd always stop and say hello. When you consider how much they're idolised by so many people, it certainly brought it home to me what a privilege it was to be playing for Manchester United.

When we played our game against FC Valur, there were fits and starts, suggestions he might do something, but where he'd once been able to get away before you could blink, he was getting tackled pretty easily – not that anyone was going in hard on him, it was pre-season after all, but George at that point was 36 anyway – even without his problems, that's an age where the mind wants to do something but the body can't always respond in kind. We won and then went on to have another pre-season game in Spain against Zaragoza; though I'd just about established myself under Ron, I was getting the impression that John Gidman was his preferred right-back, but when John picked up a knock, that presented a big opportunity to make that position my own and it was one I wasn't going to turn down.

Spain proved a fairly good preparation destination; Jim McGregor, who was now our physio, had been telling us to take in lots of fluids. You think 'yeah of course', but Jim had been with Northern Ireland in the World Cup in Spain so was aware of the dangers of the climate and how best to prepare. Jim was stressing to us that we ought to take in so much prior to the games that we almost felt uncomfortable as within ten minutes of kick-off it would all be used up anyway; it was advice that I took on board and that helped continue my good pre-season that put me in a good position to be starting when the serious business kicked off. On the subject of physiotherapists, part of our pre-season included a testimonial match in memory of Jim Headridge, the physio who had sadly died at The Cliff the previous year.

Someone who had been with Jim was of course Norman Whiteside. Norman had made a name for himself with Northern Ireland by becoming the youngest ever player at a World Cup and I must confess I was a little envious of him over the summer. To play in a World Cup was such an achievement but it reinforced my hope and belief that I could one day take part in one too – he, like me, was just a normal lad from Manchester United. He'd certainly made a contribution back at Old Trafford though; coming to attention at the end of the previous season, he was flying in pre-season too and grabbed a couple in a testimonial for Don Givens over in Ireland.

That season we had a bit of a competition within the team where we would mark off our appearances on the fixture list for whether we'd played in it or not. Norman played 57 times that year and I just beat him with 60 – it was about the only thing I got over him, though with goals in the cup finals, I'm sure Norman had plenty of consolation!

In the 1982/83 season I would make more appearances for Manchester United than any other player, normally at right-back, though even after all this time it's a tough one when I'm asked what my favourite position in the team was. As someone who played in a number of different positions my memories are drawn more to 'good games' that I had in different roles. Early on in my career though I suppose it would be fair to say right-back was the role I'd seen as 'mine' in the team, the role I felt most comfortable in. I was relied on to defend but was also given licence to attack; later on, I think I preferred centre-half. Centre-half was a lot more demanding mentally than full-back but as you get older you deal with that better. I suppose, with the anxiety I'd felt with John Gidman's arrival more than any others, that at least on some subconscious level I felt that was my best chance of getting in the team.

We had a buoyant start to the First Division season, winning four of our first five games, with Norman scoring four goals. Norman had replaced me as the youngest member of the team but there was a youthful feel about us, as if we were a team on the road to its collective peak. Previously I'd felt on the periphery but by now it was 'us', very much a United team that I felt a part of. Sadly that togetherness and good form didn't hold up for us in Europe – our league place had seen us qualify for the UEFA Cup but we went out in the first round against a good Valencia side that had Mario Kempes. To be fair, we were second best in the tie – there was obvious disappointment but we could have no complaints when we were beaten 2-1 in the return leg out in Spain after a draw at home. You have to beat the very best teams in order to win the big trophies so we weren't daunted by it – yet a casual look at the names that United had encountered since returning to Europe in 1976 (Juventus, Ajax, and now Valencia) showed that perhaps the early round exits were a little more understandable than they first appeared.

When you're getting that kind of opponent as your first on the continent then it's difficult to properly gain the kind of European experience that is so vital – and unlike how it is these days with the group stages in almost every European competition, these were straightforward two-legged ties against one opponent. There was no room for a bad result or a hiccup. Maybe we needed one or two smaller opponents to ease our way in.

I did enjoy some success abroad the following month, October 1982 and that was with the England under-21s. I was now 23 but continued to feature as I had been of the right age when the European Championships began; Gary Owen and Sammy Lee were our overage players which we were allowed. I'd played in the group stages but I didn't play any part in the quarter-finals or semi-finals yet was recalled to face West Germany in the final. In the first leg we won 3-1 at Bramall Lane – Owen getting two and Justin Fashanu scoring the other. That put us in a great position for the second leg in Bremen where we narrowly lost 3-2 with Pierre Littbarski scoring a hat-trick. I scored what turned out to be a vital goal in that game – picking the ball up on halfway, playing a one-two and then slipping it past the keeper – but we were hanging on at the end, just managing to clinch an aggregate win.

We had a great night out afterwards in Bremen to celebrate. I remember Dave Sexton, who was managing us, motivating us before the games doing his best Clive Dunn impression from *Dad's Army*, 'They don't like it up 'em!' It wasn't meant disrespectfully, it was simply meant as a rallying cry and it certainly did the trick as we won. There had been a historical rivalry with England and West Germany in football going back to the World Cup and for me as an Englishman to score in a final against them was very special. Well, just for me as Mick Duxbury to score in a game was very special as it's something that didn't happen a lot! And at any level, to win a trophy with your country is a very proud moment in your life.

It's a great honour to play for the under-21s and comes with its own set of pressures and circumstances. You don't get the crowds of the first team; dare I say it, it almost felt like a reserve team fixture. Not that I want to do a disservice to the under-21s but until you got to the final there was no real pressure to win, the emphasis was on development. Perhaps it made it a bit easier – there was certainly the same level of pride that went into representing England for me, particularly as I'd missed out on the previous levels. I thoroughly enjoyed playing at that level but felt that when my senior call-up finally came it was a step too much, which is something I'll discuss at length a bit later on.

The win came at a good time; I felt I was playing some of the best football of my life and looking back it was probably the best I ever played. With the two cup runs, it's a year remembered fondly by United supporters too, and our Milk Cup campaign got off to a good start when we comfortably knocked out Bournemouth in the second round.

Just as with Brighton, Bournemouth would be a side we'd see again in more famous – or should I say infamous – circumstances but the most notable thing about this encounter was the sole appearance of Peter Beardsley for Manchester United. Peter had been at the club for a little while; I would sit and have a chat with him about what was in the papers in the morning and he seemed to be settling in. With what Peter went on to achieve afterwards he's always seen as one who 'got away' but to be perfectly honest, aside from a few glimpses in training, there didn't seem to be an awful lot there at the time that suggested he could have been a big success at United and so it was understandable he wasn't kept for longer – like I say, at the time, anyway!

Even in that Milk Cup game he didn't do anything remarkable. That might be unfair as he could have perhaps done with a few more matches before you could properly judge his ability but I don't think at the time there was much of an argument about the decision to let him go. That isn't anything bad about Peter's ability – some players just flourish in different environments, and though their personal circumstances are probably worlds apart, one only has to look at Ravel Morrison for a player with all the ability in the world but one better suited away from Old Trafford.

Cup runs are great but at Manchester United we all had a strong desire to be the first United side to win the league since 1967 and we'd started in great fashion – in a tight division, that early defeat was the only one until we lost at the Boleyn Ground in the last weekend of October following draws with Liverpool and Manchester City. We were now third, behind Liverpool and West Ham who had moved ahead of us on goal difference with that win. Our problem wasn't getting results against the likes of Liverpool, it was getting them in the so-called smaller games, and that was proved again as the week after the West Ham defeat we lost 1-0 at Brighton. It was that inconsistency that would often get levelled at us and what ultimately cost us, too, but we went into every game with the expectation that we would win it.

We picked up our form with three consecutive wins, the last of which was a 4-0 victory over Notts County where I managed to net my only United goal of the season. It must have been a theme of how I would score goals in 1982 but I intercepted a ball around the halfway line, played a one-two with Norman and then I think the ball just bobbled in off my shin. I'd got in to the box, and I don't know if I was panicking or what – knowing me, I probably was – but the ball bobbled and I think I shinned it in. All the lads came up and started taking the mick out of me for it – crazy that we could be having this intimate chat about what had gone on in front of 60,000 people! They couldn't just celebrate, they had to take the mick!

That 4-0 win was how I think most people remember us that season; entertaining, and plenty of goals, but maybe we should have saved some as we went three of the next four games without scoring. Three goalless draws and a defeat at Coventry in the last league game of 1982 meant that we went into the FA Cup third round game with West Ham ten points behind a Liverpool team who looked formidable and were scoring plenty of goals, particularly at home.

Our home form was good too but we were just plagued by the inconsistency which to my mind was largely unexplainable. If there's one thing you could never accuse us of with Bryan Robson as captain, it was complacency. And, looking around the squad, I felt that we were more than capable of achieving more than we ultimately would in the league. I suppose that's the beauty of football, that things that shouldn't be just happen, fairytales and giant-killings that just seem unfathomable. Not that it was something we considered beautiful at the time, I hasten to add! Knocking out West Ham in the cup was the first of five consecutive wins, though only two were in the league – our 4-0 hammering of Nottingham Forest in the Milk Cup quarter-final set up a semi-final clash with Arsenal and I think that was the first time we as a group of players began to get the smell of Wembley.

Confidence was sky high both collectively and personally – I was enjoying myself more than ever and that was partly down to the run I was getting in the team. The only period of football I missed at all in the season was in the FA Cup quarter-final when I was substituted. We were facing Everton at Old Trafford and the game was 0-0 going into the closing stages and Ron brought Lou Macari on for me with two minutes remaining. I asked Ron right away, 'Why did you take me off?' He said it was because I was the nearest player, which would have been okay if I hadn't literally just walked past three players to come off. I was at right-back and we were attacking the Stretford End – I couldn't have been further away! I would have taken any excuse but to just blatantly lie was ridiculous. Frank Stapleton scored and we ended up winning; so how could I really complain? I missed two minutes of the entire season, though, those two minutes, and it was something that stuck with me for a little while, I have to admit.

Ron had been at the club for nearly two years but my initial reservations about his personality had never completely gone away. He would say things and rant and rave sometimes but I could never quite tell if it was serious or bravado. He would have a go at me for the way that I would open my body up to receive the ball from the goalkeeper – it was just something I naturally did, I would knock the ball with the outside of my foot and then I'd be away. It was a natural movement to keep the ball flowing so I thought it was a good thing to do; it's something I've seen a lot of successful full-backs do in recent years. In training, it was becoming more and more like he was setting it up for himself sometimes. All managers joined in the five-a-sides but he'd still be participating in the drills which was not only pointless from his side but also potentially doing us more harm. He wasn't going to be on the pitch on a Saturday, after all.

In general training would be okay and enjoyable; it was never dull, and never too much hard work. I don't know how much of that perception was because everything seemed to be going right on the field but any doubts I did have on the manager were not enough to influence my feeling of being at the club at that time. I was able to separate the two feelings – in fairness, I'd done that pretty much as soon as Ron had brought in John as that immediately suggested I wouldn't be his 'first choice' – and it was probably for the best that I did that. I don't know if Ron's occasional pop at me was because I was an easy target, someone who wasn't a superstar in the team, as I wouldn't necessarily argue back with him either.

My answer had to be my form and I was playing so well that I had to be first choice – it's easier to play in a winning team, of course, and you probably learn a lot more about a team when they're getting beat. We'd had our share of disappointments that season alone but we were feeling positive with the momentum generated by the cup runs – the Everton cup game came just before the League Cup Final against Liverpool, which we had qualified for after a memorable semi-final with Arsenal.

We went to Highbury and came away with a comprehensive 4-2 victory but you wouldn't have thought that in the dressing room afterwards, we were gutted! It was a freezing cold night; we reckoned these 'soft southern lot' weren't up for it. We changed the studs – we were used to wearing rubber, but we put some old studs in that had more of a grip on the pitch. I'm not sure whether the studs made a difference but we absolutely battered them – I think we were either 4-0 up, or 4-1, and in the end we were gutted that it finished 4-2.

It sounds stupid, but we were honestly deflated. If anyone would have told us that would be the scoreline before, or that we'd win 2-0 for example, we'd have taken it every day of the week. Perhaps it's simply because the performance from the team – with Frank and Norman getting a goal each and Stevie Coppell grabbing a brace – deserved so much more than a two-goal cushion. It's funny how winning in such a style can still leave you deflated.

It's equally funny that I write this the day after my school team won away at Stockport Grammar – we were 6-0 up at one stage, then they got back to 6-4 before we scored a seventh to seal the game. They were a decent side and it was a fantastic win but you still feel as if something was missing. I suppose that's part and parcel of the mentality of being at United – you then address the problems, why did they come back, was there a moment of complacency there? There was a similar occasion in the 1998 FA Cup when United went 5-0 up at Chelsea and that finished 5-3. I suppose it's a good problem to have. Over the years United have proven themselves to be as good as anyone at seizing on complacency in other teams' leads to get famous comebacks.

Being an ever-present that season, my 100th appearance for United came early in 1983 – though not quite as memorable as my 99th, which had been that game at Highbury. Game 100 was the FA Cup win at Derby which set up that quarter-final against Everton. It wasn't a vintage performance; we had a scare at the end but I timed a tackle just right to help us see the game out. It was nothing brilliant, and the Baseball Ground in the winter wasn't going to be great, but we did the job. Game 101 was the return against Arsenal and it was always going to be very difficult for it to live up to the first leg, and it was just as well it didn't for us. Stevie scored again in what would turn out to be his last 'big game' winner for us, as we secured a final place. There was a sense of slight disappointment it hadn't been as good as the first leg but it was a real achievement to get to Wembley. There was only Stevie and Arthur who remained in the first team from the 1977 final.

Another player nearing the end of a long spell at Old Trafford, who had also been around in 1977 but was not likely to feature in any games of importance, was Martin Buchan. As a footballer, you're not programmed for being 'phased out', though there is an acceptance that it will one day happen. It doesn't make it any easier when it does; we were delighted for Kevin Moran who had come in and done remarkably well in Martin's place but we were also disappointed for Martin who for one reason or another was coming to the end of his career. It's worse for the player who's coming in – I remember shortly after Sir Alex came in, that I took over from Arthur at left-back, and that hit me a lot harder than it would if it had either been a new left-back coming in and not doing so well or anybody other than someone I'd played alongside for so many games. Arthur was such a stalwart at the club and never let anybody down yet I was moved there as part of his phasing out; it's just part of footballing life, however.

People's memories of Martin are of him being a world-class defender and it was a shame for his final season to be so fragmented but I think there was a clash of personalities between him and Ron, as you might imagine. That's not making any excuses, it doesn't make it right nor does it gloss over the fact that Martin was naturally nearing the end anyway, but perhaps the relationship between the two meant that Martin didn't get the number of games he might have under someone else. It wasn't just Kevin, but Paul McGrath had joined the club and was showing some real promise in training. He took a little while to integrate as he was very shy at first; for such a big lad, he had great feet and ability on the ball.

If you'd asked me at the time if the cup runs were taking our attention away from the league I'd have put my hand on my heart and said no, but now, looking back I really don't know. I'd like to think not; having a good run in the cup didn't mean you had to play poorly in the league, and at Manchester United you can't afford to think like that anyway or your very position in the

team will be at risk. What I can say for definite is that it was a
new challenge for us to be involved in the cups at this late stage
and perhaps that's what took its toll on our form in the league.
Look at United in recent years and they're used to competing
on all fronts at the end of the season; there are no excuses as
all clubs have to deal with the same thing, but maybe our squad
wasn't strong enough in number to sustain such a run without
something giving. Such hypothesising was almost worthwhile
when it came to it – heading into the League Cup Final, we were
16 points behind our opponents on the day.

Manchester United versus Liverpool in a cup final at
Wembley is up there with any fixture Britain has to offer and
I myself had experienced one as a young United player, of
course. I had hopes that my experiences of this grand stadium
as a player would be far better than those I'd had when I was
a spectator. And matchday is a lot different on the inside than
it is on the outside – for a start, we only got to the stadium
itself about an hour before kick-off. Everyone is telling you
when the day is coming up to remember to take it in and it's
easier said than done; likewise the mentality of taking every
game at a time. You try and see it as just another game, but
there is an inevitability that the occasion does creep into the
consciousness of players and maybe that serves as a leveller
for both teams.

For me, I attempted to keep it 'business as usual' and in line
with my usual superstition I got ready just the way I did for any
other match. Tie off, shirt off, methodical, reinforcing what
works for you on an everyday basis – everything you can do
to make it as normal as possible. I had plenty of superstitions
and Big Norm used to take the mick quite a bit. My average
preparation for a Saturday home game would begin on the
Friday lunchtime after training. I'd go home and literally just
blank everyone – apart from Karen! But if the phone would

ring, I wouldn't 'be in', if the door went, if the milkman came, Karen would always answer. I suppose that was me entering tunnel vision.

Ron Atkinson had more or less done away with the tradition of going to Mottram Hall which had existed previously so I would head to Old Trafford early on matchday. I'd arrive at 11.30am for the pre-match meal, then afterwards go down to the players' lounge. Other players would go elsewhere and mill around, but I would stay in there, watch *Football Focus*, some of the lads might want the racing on. We'd basically be killing time at that point – you'd deal with the odd request for autographs and so on – but it was all about settling the nerves. There was no official call to go into the dressing room to get ready for the match and Louie Macari was known to stay watching the races until about ten to three!

I can remember once being injured for a game with Liverpool and Lou and Alan Hansen were still in there at ten to. That worked for them but not for me – I'd make my way into the dressing room at five to two and be clock-watching. At the stroke of 2pm my tie went off, then my jacket, and everything was always in the same order. The same shoe off first, and then the same way putting the kit on. Nowadays the team goes out and warms up together but we all had our own routine. I would warm up in the showers near where the bath area was and do my own thing. The referee's bell went at ten to three then we'd all get ready to go out – it was that which probably got a few players racing back to get ready! When heading on to the pitch I always made sure I was third in line behind the captain and the goalkeeper. The tunnel came out of the halfway line then and there would be many well-wishers as we went out; even at that point I was still blanking people, concentrating on following the same routine.

On the pitch I'd jump up and down two or three times, and get myself ready. For me it tended to work – though I didn't ever know if it was the 'right' thing to do and I'd still get anxious occasionally. What if the milkman had wanted to see me, or if there was a really important call from someone insisting they had to speak to me? I used to hate people asking for tickets that didn't go regularly – my dad would go, as would Karen, but when someone new asked it wasn't so much the fact that they'd asked but more to do with it being their first time and the break of that superstition. It might have been a bit better if I'd had been a bit more open and relaxed!

For a cup final it was exactly the same, well, as much as you can. I don't want to sound blasé but having been used to playing in front of 50,000 and more at Old Trafford and having experienced a United and Liverpool cup final before I at least knew what I was in store for with regards the atmosphere. There were nerves but as a kid this was why you wanted to play football in the first place. The nerves are mostly the night before and start to fade once it gets past 2pm and you can get 'in the zone'. We were well aware that United hadn't won a trophy since that 1977 final against Liverpool but we got off to the best possible start when Norman scored for us with little more than ten minutes played.

It was never going to be easy though and they came back into it and put us under plenty of pressure – it just felt at times as if the game was running away from us and they had all the momentum. Kevin Moran was injured near the end, causing a defensive reshuffle as Lou Macari came on, and whether it was for that reason or another, less than five minutes later Alan Kennedy equalised with a shot that horribly bobbled in and the game went into extra time. There were a couple of moments where Bruce Grobbelaar lost his head and he might well have been sent off in today's game but he stayed on. Ronnie Whelan's goal to win it was a great way to win the final and I think, on the day, we could have no complaints about losing to a better team.

We were desperately missing Bryan Robson through injury and although I'm not making excuses, any team who had a player like that as their leader and then didn't have them for such a huge game were always going to feel the loss. You remember these things as they are the instances that are replayed and remembered yet despite the best of intentions that first cup final does pass you by and I can remember little about my own performance that day. Following that, I resolved to make more of an effort to remember the FA Cup Final should we be lucky enough to get there.

It wasn't going to be easy. As seems to be the theme about the same teams popping up in cup competitions, so it was when our reward for the FA Cup quarter-final win over Everton was a semi-final at Villa Park against Arsenal. With all due respect to Highbury and Old Trafford, there is something completely different about playing an FA Cup semi-final at a neutral venue. The FA Cup and the League Cup always differed in that the latter had plenty of two-legged rounds; not so in the former. Semi-final day in the FA Cup was a special one in the English football calendar yet we were still suffering something of a hangover from the defeat in the Milk Cup Final. There was nothing we could do but train right and try and put it right on the day – there was no point dwelling on the defeat, yes you can analyse it and see what went wrong, but come Saturday night or Sunday morning you need to be thinking about the next game.

One thing we definitely had going in our favour was the return of Bryan Robson and that proved crucial but just as influential on the day was Norman Whiteside. He wasn't yet 18 but he had the physique of a fully-grown man and he was a constant menace for the Arsenal defence all afternoon. Things didn't start great for us as Gary Bailey made a big error and Tony Woodcock put the ball in from on the line. It was Robson and Whiteside to the rescue – Bryan scored a smart goal just after half-time but Norman's winner midway through the second half was a real thunderbolt. The goal was enough to give us our second Wembley visit in just a few weeks and a chance to put behind us the loss against Liverpool.

Our opponents would be Brighton – the team I'd scored my first United goal against, and the team who we'd faced the previous year in the FA Cup too. We couldn't underestimate them and say, 'Oh it's only Brighton.' After all, Southampton were in the Second Division when they famously beat United in 1976 and furthermore, Brighton had beaten us already earlier in the season so had proven themselves formidable opposition. In 1976 the United lads had a year to brood over putting it right but at least we had a very quick opportunity to do ourselves justice.

We hadn't done that in the league. After the Arsenal match we were a massive 21 points behind Liverpool though we had three games in hand. We were still unbeaten at Old Trafford – and would win all our remaining home games as well – but it was draws that ultimately cost us. There could be no denying that Liverpool were worthy champions but, at that time, we'd lost just six times while Watford, in second, had lost 13. They finished with 15 losses and with nothing to play for we lost all but one of our remaining away games, finishing with ten defeats. None of the top teams covered themselves in glory in the run-in with even Liverpool, with the guarantee of the First Division title no matter what, picking up just one point in their last five fixtures. Even with that form we could have won all of our remaining games and not won the league.

For the first time I considered that maybe the lack of a true top-class goalkeeper was partly responsible for our lack of a real challenge. I liked Gary Bailey but he was prone to an error; we'd gotten away with it against Arsenal but over a long league campaign there is no place to hide. Brian Clough once spoke about the value of a class goalkeeper being worth ten to 12 points a season – there had been talk of Peter Shilton joining United when Tommy Docherty was in charge and the same kind of speculation often made the press now, years later. That said, our home form was just about the best in the division – no defeats, and the best defensive record. It was Ron Atkinson's job now to figure out the million-dollar question of how to turn the potential into a title-winning machine.

First of all, of course, was the not-quite-so-insignificant matter of the FA Cup Final. Just like semi-final day, FA Cup Final day really held special interest in England, so much so that there was a full day of television broadcasting dedicated to it. It was something I'd watched myself over and over again, sat on the settee at home and enjoyed all the build-up. It took some getting used to on the other side, though. We had the ITV crew with us as the BBC cameras were with Brighton and Jim Rosenthal was hosting their coverage. Me and Ray Wilkins were sat having our breakfast when the cameras came up and I was thinking, 'Oh God.' Jim said to us, 'So this is just a normal breakfast for you boys?'

Yeah Jim, we always have the cameras following us around! I was going to say that, but I bottled it! It was my first thought, but then you end up just mumbling and agreeing, but I regret not saying that.

Tradition plays a big part and with the FA Cup there are long-running institutional superstitions that collide with your own. The most successful dressing room, the hotel that the club stays in, and so on. As you head in to the dressing rooms, I seem to recall that the 'charmed' dressing room was the one on the left. Brighton were on the right. People mention the superstition but then you think, 'Well, today's just another day.' It quickly becomes apparent that it's not, though, when you're trying to get on with things and then you keep receiving telegrams from people wishing you well, people you've not seen in years! I got one from the deputy head of my old school and even from someone Karen and I had once met on holiday. You can't just leave them, though I might have if I'd have had the option! Again, no disrespect intended to anyone who sent one, but it was interrupting my preparation. I did keep them, to be fair, my mum has still got them. I do keep things but I'm not a hoarder.

It brings to mind an interview I once saw on television where former Arsenal striker Ian Wright was talking to his old team-mate Emmanuel Petit. Emmanuel shared a story about how he'd lost a brother earlier in his life – apparently his brother was a talented player too – and the conversation naturally evolved into the World Cup that he had won with France. Ian asked him where his medal was and was incredulous to discover that Petit did not know; he said that he would rather have his brother back than have the medal. It wasn't that he didn't appreciate his achievement, he did, but more for the achievement itself than the physical award of gold afterwards, and I must say that was something that really resonated with myself. I was lucky enough to win two FA Cup medals and I know where they both are but I haven't seen them for years. They'll go to my sons, but I've already said if they want to sell them, they can.

Speaking of mementoes, we didn't often get to keep our shirts either; but the club made an exception for the 1983 FA Cup Final and somehow we also ended up with a Brighton shirt each too. Both teams, I think, had a set of each other's. We left them at Old Trafford and Norman Davies locked up as he always did – the club was broken into that night and all the shirts got nicked! After that, the club got our shirts remade, but not the Brighton ones. Four hundred games and the only shirts I've got are a replica of the 1983 FA Cup Final and my 1985 FA Cup Final shirt.

Have I spoiled what comes next? Going back to the point about us not taking Brighton lightly, there was certainly no chance of that. We hadn't scored against them in the league that year and when Gordon Smith scored early on in the final, we were aware of just how tough it was going to be. We didn't start great but came back into it and were probably the better side for most of the game – for a period in the second half we made our dominance pay when Frank Stapleton equalised and then quarter of an hour later, Ray Wilkins scored a goal not too dissimilar to the one Ronnie Whelan scored against us. Ray wasn't prolific but that was a beauty and he certainly enjoyed celebrating it. He was over the hoardings and on to the greyhound track as quick as anything!

Gary Stevens scored with just three minutes remaining and in extra time, Smith famously missed an opportunity to win the game for them. I was treading water at that point on a dreadful pitch and I can remember clearly that Ray and myself just couldn't get back to it – every time I watch it back I think, 'How did Gary save that?' It was easier to score to be fair and I'm sure Gordon thinks that every time he thinks of it too.

There was tremendous relief when he didn't score and the whistle blew for full time. For Gary it was certainly a great moment – like I've said, I felt that maybe we were a top-class keeper away from being a real contender, or at least making the difference, but no-one could begrudge Gary that moment. At that time, the most famous save in United's history had been Alex Stepney's in the European Cup Final in 1968 to deny Eusebio what would have been a certain winner at the end of normal time. Gary had not only replicated it at the same stadium but in front of the same goal.

It was a dream save for Gary. Likewise, everyone dreams of scoring a goal at Wembley; there wasn't so much emphasis on the great providers back then as statistics had only started to be discussed with regards 'assists' – if you were to look back over the 1982/83 season, I'm certain that I would have been up there near the top of United's assists, and I was pleased that I was able to make a contribution in the final as it was my ball in that Frank got our equaliser from. I'd combined with Alan Davies, a young Welsh player, in the build-up for the goal, and Alan had only got his place in the team because of the forced retirement of Stevie Coppell earlier in the campaign.

Stevie was a huge loss to the team, particularly as he'd take the young players under his wing; he did that with Norman, offering advice and try and help you out in training too. Be it personal or financial, Stevie was a wonderfully approachable person and as a winger he was the ideal player to be a full-back behind. I said it earlier, one man's crisis is another's opportunity and so it was for Alan; it didn't faze him, he was a bubbly lad who could take everything in his stride. There was an element of tragedy all around with that position following Stevie's retirement as Laurie Cunningham was signed on loan to replace him on a short-term basis. Laurie picked up an injury just before the final and was asked if he wanted to play and he said no.

I don't know if I could have done that even if I was really hurt – I couldn't turn down the chance to play in a cup final.

As exhausted as I'd been at the end of extra time there was no way I wouldn't be featuring in the replay.

We were unchanged, but Brighton made a selection gamble – Steve Foster was their captain, an iconic figure who wore a sweatband on his head. He'd missed the first game and Gary Stevens, who'd played in the centre in his place, put in a marvellous performance. Foster was recalled despite not really being fit. It was a sentimental decision that meant Stevens was moved out of position and it backfired for them quite spectacularly.

One person who I certainly did have sympathy for was a player who missed the final altogether, Remi Moses, who I'd gotten really close with in the two years he'd been at United. He'd been sent off in a league game against Arsenal so was suspended and to be fair I think there was a little bit of afters from the semi-final that had led to it. I didn't feel the challenge he was sent off for warranted it but what was done was done; years later, I too would suffer the blow of a cup final decision not made on sentiment.

With Brighton misshapen, from the off, we were on it and by half-time we'd blown them away – our semi-final heroes Robson and Whiteside scoring again, and just before the break Bryan scored once more to seal the result. We had to guard against the kind of complacency that we'd showed temporarily in the first Arsenal semi-final but at half-time I couldn't help but feel there was a lack of impetus left in the occasion. There's a little bit of uncertainty; you know the game isn't won after 45 minutes but with it not being quite as competitive as the second half, the final whistle wasn't quite as euphoric as it might have been if the game had been a little tighter. We scored a fourth in the second half when Arnie Muhren converted from the penalty spot. With Bryan on a hat-trick, it was strange he didn't take it. It didn't quite sink in that we'd won the cup until I was walking up the stairs to collect my medal and hold the trophy; we went straight back to Manchester following the game and the celebrations continued into the night.

7

Recollections

AMID the happiness of May 1983 was a fairly significant amount of personal and professional tragedy, some of which I have already touched on – not for me, as the 1982/83 season was probably the best I'd played as a professional, but for a number of my team-mates.

There was Stevie Coppell who retired – he had been injured on England duty and never quite recovered to be fully comfortable playing again. When you look at it, although he'd been at the club since 1975, it felt like he'd been there even longer. He was only 28, and with so much of his game being about working hard, there was every reason to feel that if he had stayed injury-free I could have worked in tandem with him down that right-hand side for another four or five years. He was part of the furniture and he was at his peak – there's never a good time for something like that to happen, but it's even worse when it comes at a time when you're supposed to have your best years ahead of you.

As I've said, he was great to have around the club and was really helpful with the younger players – he was renowned as a quiet, studious kind of person and I always got on with him.

As a player and person he was going to be missed at Old Trafford, there's no doubt about that in my mind. Steve went on to become a manager and did a really good job at Crystal Palace before an infamous short spell at Manchester City. He resigned after 33 days through stress and that surprised me as I never thought that he was the kind of person who was affected by that sort of thing. I don't know the ins and outs of it but it was surprising considering how helpful he was.

Stevie's retirement meant there was only Arthur Albiston and Lou Macari left as regulars from the 1977 FA Cup-winning side and six years is a pretty short amount of time to essentially have a turnaround of nine first-team players. Martin Buchan was still at the club but his time would shortly be coming to an end. Management changes always have an effect when considering the players they bring in but even so, for such a young side to be no longer was surprising.

When you look at the players from that side and where they were in 1983 after leaving United, Sammy McIlroy who had been sold soon after Ron Atkinson's arrival, and now Stevie, it was an incredible loss of talent. It sounds harsh to say it but that's football; Tommy Docherty's sacking was the catalyst for it all.

You have an understanding of some departures but I can't really comment as I wasn't a part of that team as such – whereas a year after the 1983 FA Cup Final (though I'm jumping ahead of time!) Ron sold Ray Wilkins and I felt that was a tremendous loss. I remember when he came back with QPR and in the warm-up I went over and told him we should never have let him go. For Ray, though, it was a wonderful opportunity to go to Milan at that time, not least in a financial sense. In those days, Italian football was admired as one of the best leagues and that was seen as the place to be, as people see the Premier League these days. It was a very lucrative move and you could understand that – I felt the solitary FA Cup winner's medal he won in 1983 didn't reflect his quality and contribution at Manchester United.

Martin Buchan's departure from United was more conventionally straightforward in that he was coming towards the end of his career but to be completely honest I feel there has to be some value in keeping a player of his experience around. I don't know if I'm speaking out of turn with that as he never went into management or coaching so maybe it just wasn't for him but I thought he was a shining example to the younger players at the club and a marvellous captain.

The professional tragedy of Steve was followed by the personal tragedy of his replacement in the FA Cup Final, Alan Davies. Following his good performance in the 1983 final Alan still had plenty of good displays left in him at United, as I'll discuss later. Sadly it quietened down for him at the club and he didn't quite make the mark he could have in the game – he had a couple of spells at Swansea and he also went to Bradford City but in 1992 I was saddened to hear that he'd taken his own life at the young age of 30. I think I was at Blackburn at the time and I went to the funeral – he was married with children, such a terrible tragedy. There were a few United lads at the funeral, Stuart Pearson, and Dave Haggart who, of course, I knew from my days as a kid at the club. He drove up from south Wales – I think he's a chief inspector in the police now. For it all to end for Alan like that was tragic, particularly after the highs that we all shared in 1983.

I was still only young but I'm not sure that it ever got any better for me than it was in 1983. I'd already come a long way and I felt appreciative of that journey because it had taken a lot of hard work to get there. I had played so well and so often and to do that in a team that was doing well was even better. Okay, so we had come up short in the league, but to get to one cup final and win another was progress in anyone's mind. Some might say that finishing third in the league was just as well as we'd done for a while but losing four out of our last eight games saw us drop off. We should definitely at least have finished second and done so comfortably. The success in other areas meant that we didn't approach moving forward with disappointment; it had been the club's best season since 1968 and so for that reason we were all looking to go one better. If anyone was to look at the reasons for why we didn't win more than we did then they couldn't put it down to attitude – we were motivated by the disappointment of coming up short in the league and losing the League Cup Final.

Other clubs might view such a season as a hugely successful one but for us, it was a building block for the next step. I can't speak for other players but I would always hope that such an outlook was shared by everyone. What had been was great but it was the past and it was time to move on. We were pleased, but not satisfied, is probably the best way of describing it.

Before we could concentrate on the new season, however, we still had to close out the old one with a post-season tour to Swaziland where it had been arranged that we would play Tottenham Hotspur twice. We had a good trip. I roomed with Remi and he really enjoyed the trip – to be in Africa (although I suppose it was a little different in Swaziland) was something he appeared to treat as a spiritual homecoming and it was pleasing to see. Some of the lads went on the safari trips and we played a couple of informal games against local teams before the organised friendlies against Spurs.

We also played a local select XI in a combined team with Spurs, and I was one of the players selected to represent United. Afterwards, there was a presentation where the players were given a Krugerrand to commemorate their participation. For whatever reason, I didn't get one – I came on as a sub, so maybe they were only given to the starters – it seemed very strange.

It is difficult to give an honest impression of Africa because again, we were restricted to the structure and activities that had been planned out and going out and exploring was not exactly encouraged by anyone given the political climate at the time. We always stayed – normally, anyway – at top hotels so I was very grateful at the time and I wouldn't wish to sound ungrateful now but sometimes, like when we were in Africa this time, I would later reflect and say that although I'd been there I didn't really feel like I'd seen so much. It was an experience to visit there regardless, even if it did end disappointingly with a defeat to Spurs in our last game.

After being in Swaziland, we flew down to Johannesburg to spend a couple of days there, but again, we didn't see much outside of Sun City. As we arrived at the hotel I received a message from my cousin to say that he was staying at the same place, and he invited me for a drink. He'd been out there for a while and asked me if I wanted to go out and see the local area – so I was fortunate that I at least got to see a little bit of the country that I normally wouldn't have.

I'd played as many games as I would in a season so after the trip I took what I felt was a well-earned break and literally did nothing and went nowhere over the summer! There was a transitional period for the landscape of English football; Bob Paisley retired after a successful spell at Liverpool and was replaced by Joe Fagan. Given the continuity that the club had enjoyed from Shankly to Paisley there was never any thought that it would be any different this time around and we assumed it would be a smooth transition. We weren't counting on it, at least. Whether it was Paisley, Fagan or whoever, our main ambition was to improve ourselves and we were focusing on that rather than other clubs. As it transpired, we'd be pitting our wits directly against our north-west rivals as part of our preparation for a season where we were hoping to overtake them.

8

From Bournemouth To Barcelona

ARTHUR Graham was the only addition in the early weeks of the 1983/84 season – the summer had seen us lose Buchan, Cunningham and Ashley Grimes. Arthur's best days had been behind him, too – at 32, he was never really likely to be a long-term option for the left wing, but his experience suggested he would be a reliable, consistent name, and maybe that's what Ron was considering when spending £50,000 to bring him from Leeds United. With all due respect, he was probably very much a stop-gap signing. He was a lovely lad, not quite at Stevie's level, but you could always give him the ball. Calling him a stop-gap might sound like I'm being detrimental to him because he served a purpose and I never really felt he struggled at the club.

He certainly didn't on his debut – applying himself accordingly against Liverpool, who provided a major test in a testimonial for IFA secretary Bill Drennan. We took some time to get going and Liverpool scored early on but we recovered to win an entertaining game 4-3 in front of a healthy crowd of 30,000. We weren't going to take anything from that other than it being a good workout and slightly more competitive than normal. Until the sides played each other in the pre-season of the 2014/15 season I believe that is the only other time there's been a friendly game between the clubs.

This would be a year where I really would get the opportunity to play against some of the world's best but at the time it felt like I was only coming up against them in pre-season. Johan Cruyff was playing for Feyenoord in a tournament we played in Holland – we always seemed to struggle over there, and this was no different, as we lost 2-1 to Cruyff and Feyenoord and then 1-0 to Ajax. The records show that I played against Cruyff but I have no real memories of it that stand out – I should have, shouldn't I? Goodness me. Why wasn't I following him around, trying to rip his shirt off?! Not the finest thing to admit when putting my autobiography together. I'd like to think it's because I kept him so quiet it was forgettable but it's far more likely that I have tried to forget it ever happened for quite the opposite reason!

Maybe I was simply focused on my preparation for the real business and that began with the Charity Shield against Liverpool. In an ideal world we'd have strengthened our squad but simply looking at the numbers and experience that we'd lost, we were heading into the 1983/84 season a little weaker – even accounting for our year's collective development as a team. Selfishly, I was just pleased to be in the starting 11.

You would like to think that we were looking to attract top players and I'm sure we did that – in fact, I seem to recall that around the time, Ron wanted to bring in Peter Shilton, but the proposed transfer was blocked for reasons unknown to me – as far as I remember, it was down to wages. Keen historians at the club might well point out to me a case of deja vu at this point – as Tommy Docherty had tried to sign Shilton too, and had failed to do so for precisely the same reason. Shilton was 33 but still capable, as he was showing at Southampton, establishing himself as the number one for England after a long battle for the shirt with Ray Clemence. I felt we really needed a top-class goalkeeper, and the time for that had arrived.

Regardless of the lack of significant investment and improvement, we came out on top in the head-to-head with Fagan's Liverpool in the Charity Shield. As the competitive game with them recently had proved, both teams would be up for it, and with our Milk Cup defeat still fresh in our minds, we were well worthy of a 2-0 win – it was only one game but still a good result. Bryan Robson scored our goals, to underline his importance and remind everyone that he could well have tipped the balance in our favour in the Milk Cup Final if he had been available.

We started the league season with two home games – winning one, against QPR, and then losing the next against Nottingham Forest. I picked up an injury which meant I missed the next three league matches, which were all won, to put us in a strong position at the start of the campaign.

I returned to the team for the European Cup Winners' Cup tie against Dukla Prague at Old Trafford – we had to rely on a late Ray Wilkins goal to salvage a draw and preserve the club's unbeaten home record in Europe. I'd been aware of the record ever since the club had been forced to play at Plymouth against St Etienne and there was talk about whether or not it would count as the record being lost if we had been defeated. We achieved a 2-2 draw in Prague to go through.

If ever you wanted to perform a study in just why our United team failed to win a league title in the 1980s then there'd be no better place to start than in our games against Southampton, Liverpool and Norwich City which followed the Dukla Prague home match.

We were defeated 3-0 against Southampton, then beat Liverpool, and then capitulated at Carrow Road. We were cruising – we went ahead just before half-time and then scored twice early in the second half. They made a tactical change but even on 3-0 we weren't going to shut up shop. They scored, and scored again, and our response was always to try and score again. They equalised in the last minute. One of those games, or a problem in the team that we couldn't cure? The mood in the dressing room was very poor.

Critics of the manager might have said that he was unable to instil the kind of discipline required to kill games off. Ron Atkinson's mood never seemed to be consistent and when he was critical of the team, the next minute he'd be having a laugh and joke, so you wouldn't quite know if he himself took it seriously. This isn't to absolve the players of responsibility, but managers earn their corn by making tough choices, and their role in their team's performance should be praised and criticised accordingly too. Sometimes it seemed for show – and this would happen later this season too.

There was a decent response to that inconsistent period in a run of games which saw the emergence of Mark Hughes into the first team. I'd seen bits of him in training, enough to be excited that he would make an impact. It's a little surprising to hear stories of him today as a manager, going into great detail and analysing statistics, because it couldn't have been more different to how he was in those early days as a player. He would come out for the warm-up and the first thing he'd be doing was attempting volleys from the halfway line. I couldn't understand it, it took about half an hour of a warm-up for me to just get myself moving! He'd be smashing balls all over the place and that was exactly as he was when the 90 minutes started. He could handle himself and it was good to see another young lad break in. Graeme Hogg got through at the same time – and they shared digs together. It used to make us laugh because they lived the closest but were always last in to training.

We qualified for the third round of the Cup Winners' Cup (effectively the quarter-final) by eliminating Spartak Varna with comfortable wins in both legs and at the end of November we were top of the league after a comprehensive 3-0 victory over Wolves. There was certainly a feel-good factor around the club with the players really enjoying their football and I was given the ultimate accolade in that November when I got my first England cap.

I'd been in the squad a couple of times before. There was an international the week after the Milk Cup Final the previous season and I had been included in that. We had a meal after the game at Wembley but travelled up to the Midlands to a restaurant owned by someone Ron knew. It was confusing to us as we should have gone to Manchester, and it seemed like a big show. We went back to Manchester and threw our boots in the skip. I went in the next day and there were no boots – no boots, and travelling to the England game! There was nowhere to buy a pair of boots except a warehouse called Winfields. I was on the bench for England that time and it was probably just as well I didn't play as those boots would have destroyed my feet.

I was back in for the European Championship qualifier in Luxembourg and roomed with Liverpool's Alan Kennedy. Gary Bailey was in the squad and one day we went to one of the shops – the shopkeeper was really wary of us. We weren't aware of it at the time but there had been rioting from the England fans. They must have thought we were part of it and we were going to ransack the shop. We didn't, of course, but we did ransack the opponents. I started – in my own boots – in the number two shirt, as we won 4-0. It would have been nice if it had been at Wembley but it was still pleasing to play, and I kept the mementoes afterwards such as the shirt and the programme.

Defeat against Denmark in the September meant that we couldn't qualify for the finals the following year but having finally broken through my concentration was on hopefully keeping my place with the World Cup in 1986 in mind.

To say the least, knockout disappointment followed me back to Manchester. Despite suffering two defeats and picking up only one win in five games in the league, we were keeping pace at the top of the table, but we suffered an embarrassing exit to Oxford in the League Cup after two replays. I set up Hughes – Sparky – for a goal in the first game at the Manor Ground, and afterwards I would joke to him that I made his career (a joke that continued after he got the better of me to score for Wales at international level, too). My claim to fame! The Oxford ties were tough. We really should have done better but could have no complaints because they were simply better than us on the day when it came to knocking us out in the second replay.

Then came Bournemouth. That was a blow to the ego, to say the least. We had been drawn against the south coast club in the third round of the FA Cup. There wasn't the best feeling that came from that game as we lost 2-0 on the day, which was humiliating enough, but afterwards there seemed to be a lot of ill will on their side, with their players slating us in the press and calling us big-time Charlies and so on. I don't know where they had got that impression from because we didn't behave that way in front of them and we certainly didn't have any characters like that in the team – whether they thought that of the manager is a different thing. It was disappointing because they were fellow professionals and it did rankle with me because it didn't need to be done. They thoroughly deserved to beat us on the day and we were very, very poor, but sometimes amid the romance of the cup, there are occasions such as this which aren't quite as pleasant as they're made out to be. Every dog has its day and the FA Cup is great, whether you're the victim of a giant-killing or the winner of the trophy, but I felt that the Bournemouth players at the time tried to make a lot more out of it than it was.

We had no complaints about the defeat but they carried it on afterwards. As United players we were most team's cup final anyway, but they were taking it further, taking our players down as if they'd taught us a lesson. We felt we had been sporting on the day. We could have easily said to them, 'You've had your day, but no matter what, come on, you are not going to win the FA Cup. It's not going to happen. Enjoy your day but do it right.' As you can tell, it still bugs me to this day! I would hope that the players were misquoted but it certainly stuck with us until we thankfully had the chance to put it right.

The defeat against Bournemouth hurt us all but the reaction summed up what I was saying earlier about Ron. First thing Monday morning, he sent us all running around in the gymnasium which seemed to be nothing but a token message to let off some steam. Was that really punishing us? Why weren't we working on something that went wrong on the Saturday? He didn't even come into the gym – Mick Brown did. It's not the same kind of authority. I suppose assistants need to be this way but he was very much a yes-man to Ron, and having the assistant there rather than the manager wasn't really sending a big message to us. You could see the difference in later years with Sir Alex. He was always present, and you knew where you stood with him, for better or worse.

Significant defeats, when they come, often signal change, and it was the case this time around as the Bournemouth defeat happened to be Lou Macari's last appearance for the club. Lou had been a fabulous player and was so difficult to play against in training with his own unique style. Horrid.

I had so much respect for him but I felt his time had come, and I'm sure he felt the same too. He was one heck of a character to have around the place. You knew if there was a joke or a culprit he was going to be the perpetrator. I was the victim a couple of times. As was Graeme Hogg on a mid-season trip to

Me and my older sister Anne outside my mum and dad's house. Talk about getting wear and tear out of your footwear!

Me, Louise and Anne on a day out.

Karen's mum and dad.

My mum and dad on their golden wedding anniversary.

My best signing – our wedding day in June 1982.

And 25 years later on our silver wedding.

FA Cup winner at Wembley, 1983 replay v Brighton. I kept the lid all the way back to Manchester!

1983 FA Cup Final replay versus Brighton.

1985 FA Cup Final against Everton, celebrating after the game.

FA Cup Final replay 1983. United 4 Brighton 0. Celebrating with Bryan Robson.

Looking forward to the Auld Enemy game with Arthur having both just been selected.

Auditions for 'Strictly'! England v Scotland and in direct opposition with team-mate Gordon Strachan.

Finally I got the Brazil shirt that I had always wanted. England v Brazil in the Maracana Stadium.

A rare photograph! Celebrating scoring a goal at Old Trafford with Arthur Albiston.

My first attempt at hair gel! League game v Charlton Athletic.

A really special moment. Scoring against City in the Manchester derby in a 3-0 win at Maine Road.

Fancy dress at players' Christmas party. Don't know who's with Karen!

Players' Christmas fancy dress with a slim looking Clayton Blackmore.

Ryan and Ashley messing around on their home-made swing.

Happy Valley Racecourse Hong Kong. Me, Ryan and Ashley with heavyweight boxer, Frank Bruno.

Ashley and Ryan on a junk in Aberdeen Harbour, Hong Kong outside the famous 'Jumbo' floating restaurant.

On our travels. Me and Karen in Thailand 2005.

Posing for the cameras. Ashley, Ryan and me.

Reunion dinner with my old digs mate David Haggart and captain Martin Buchan.

April 2014. Me and Karen at Ryan's wedding in the Ribble Valley.

And October of the same year in Cyprus with Ashley.

Majorca. Hoggy was as tight as anything. Sparky used to say that they'd go out on a Saturday night, he'd put his change on the bedside table, and in the morning, Hoggy had nicked it! He'd ask you out for a pint but never had any money! Anyway, on this trip, we went to Manos bar in Magaluf, which was a well-known watering hole. Lou says to Hoggy, 'How do you fancy winning £100? All you have to do is eat ten beefburgers.' He said yeah, and we all chipped in because we wanted to see it.

Lou goes to the bar and makes the order – the staff come out with a huge silver platter with the burgers on and all the trimmings. Hoggy, a big lad, takes the first and second burger, but all the time, we're bringing him pints to wash them down with. His eating pace began to slow and Lou started massaging his neck. It was like a scene from *Cool Hand Luke* with Paul Newman and the hard-boiled egg. While he's drinking, we're putting promotional flyers that we had been handed into the burgers. All sorts of things. He gets to about seven or eight and simply cannot take anymore. Because of the things we'd given him extra, he was more than worth that £100, so he got it. The entertainment was worth far more, I'll never forget it, and that was Lou – cutting your ties or socks, he'd always be doing something, but it was part and parcel of football.

The cup exit meant free weekends where we'd go away – such as to Magaluf – but we also had to play friendlies in Algeria and Tripoli. Everything about that Algeria trip was a nightmare. It was one of those places that wasn't particularly welcoming and memorable for the wrong reasons. I didn't go to Tripoli and after my experience in Algeria I was quite thankful.

Changes to the front line were happening with Lou's impending departure. A month earlier to the Bournemouth defeat, Ron had brought Garth Crooks in on loan. Garth is one of those who people look back on almost like a trivia question but at the time I felt it was a smart signing and I thought he did okay at the club, as short lived as his stay was.

Our fortunes were faring slightly better in the First Division. We thought we were doing well but we ended a few games more than just a little frustrated – we got a draw at Liverpool on 2 January but that was one of seven draws in ten games against teams we really ought to have beaten. It was those draws that were really holding us back as after 28 games we had lost just four times and were the top scorers in the division. I personally wasn't quite as good as I was the previous season but I still felt I was playing well and I, like the rest of the players, was looking forward to facing Barcelona, who we had been drawn against in Europe.

Barcelona, of course, had a certain Diego Maradona, but before that, I was receiving my second cap for England against France and another great in Michel Platini. I don't mind admitting it was an absolute nightmare.

The preparation for it had been a little off. Karen had given birth to Ashley, our first son, who had been delivered via caesarean section. She was allowed home on the premise that I would be there because I only trained and then came home – but we told the hospital a bit of a mistruth as she came home on the day I was due to travel to join up with the England team. So the midwife came around and we had to hide the suitcase under the bed. To Karen's credit, although she does like to remind me of that, she was brilliant the rest of the time. She never made any issue of me going away at weekends to play and was fine either with family or on her own.

In those early days she did really well. I went to France with the England team and I had a terrible game against Bruno Bellone, their left-winger – I had to look that up writing this book because everything was such a blur. I got Ashley a gift on the way back. I joined in where I could to bathe or feed him but my life was barely affected as Karen did most things, allowing me to focus on football.

After the game against France there had been a bit of a set-to in the hotel. I was sat in the reception with Ray Wilkins when a couple of reporters came in and joined in the conversation. We were talking about football in general, and the reporters were asking who we'd take from the Liverpool team. We got around to talking about Graeme Souness, who was a tough character but you like players like that. They asked Ray about Platini and he said although he was a great, world-class player he thought he'd struggle with a full year in the First Division. Headlines, the next day, were 'Platini could never play in England' or something like that. Ray and we should have known better but we thought it was just a conversation. Platini scored twice against us – one a free kick, which I turned and watched. It looked good for him on TV, but bad for me. International football wasn't going great. I wasn't enjoying it and it was becoming something of a monkey on my back.

Some might find it strange, then, that the forthcoming game against Barcelona was something I couldn't have looked forward to more. The pressure of playing for Manchester United at any time is great and playing against the biggest sides in the world, that pressure becomes as great as anything else you can experience in the game. It was one of the best experiences of my career to be at the Nou Camp, preparing for the game the night before. Diego Maradona was missing – I think he had suffered an ankle injury, and the first leg had just come too quickly for him – but they had great players all over their team.

We didn't think we were doing too badly – we went a goal down, but felt we were competing well. Later on, a ball came over from their left-hand side, over me, and they scored from the opportunity that was created. One goal became two and a 2-0 defeat in Europe away from home is a very unwelcome result to take back. Afterwards, Ron singled me out and had a go at me. 'Couldn't you have cut that out?!' he raged. Did he think I'd done it on purpose? Of course I would have done if I could have.

Two-nil is a different story to 1-0 and changes the complexion of the game entirely. We were almost satisfied at one but to concede the second so late on caused a lot of deflation in the dressing room afterwards. At least our recovery was positive. We won at Leicester and then absolutely battered Arsenal 4-0 in the game before the Barcelona return to go top of the league. The thing is, at United, they're always tough games, so even a trip to Leicester sees us finding our opponents at their absolute best and most committed. There's no chance of taking it easy.

On our way to an away game once, we went to see Liverpool play at Luton Town. They were playing on a Saturday and we were on the Sunday. The ground wasn't full. They nicked it late on, a result they probably didn't deserve, just as we'd probably done before and United would certainly do for years afterwards. My lasting memory of that, though, was thinking how horrible it must be to be Liverpool and not play in front of a packed house. The subsequent effect was that it was a reminder of just how fortunate I, and the rest of my team-mates, were to be playing for Manchester United. How lucky we were. And that magnified how important other teams saw their games with United.

Our own fans had all the motivation they needed for the second leg against Barcelona. With embarrassing defeats in the domestic cups and a 2-0 deficit before kick-off in this game, there was no chance that we could be patient. We would have to attack from the first minute. That was the least that the supporters expected and that's what they got. We knew, as players, that we might as well go down 5-3 as 2-0. Before the game I was suffering with flu and was asked if I was all right – as if there was any chance I was going to miss it. The atmosphere was bubbling and as soon as we scored the first, through Robson, it became unbelievable. If ever the roof was going to come off a ground, that was the night. It was absolutely manic and I'm sure that the supporters forced us to play the way we did. We didn't have a choice.

I'd played at Old Trafford so many times, as well as many other great arenas, but when the noise is like it was that night, it elevates it to another level and creates an experience beyond your dreams. It almost makes it feel like you're playing somewhere else. There were spells in games where we'd heard similar noise but this was relentless fever pitch from the first minute and it inspired us to play our part.

Comebacks aren't the specific property of Manchester United but few do it quite so significantly. Only an Old Trafford crowd could have expected a recovery on the kind of scale which is simply unprecedented. The most profound comeback was the ten-year road which Sir Matt Busby, Jimmy Murphy, Bill Foulkes and Sir Bobby Charlton travelled from Munich 1958 to Wembley 1968, but even in my time at the club as a youngster, I'd seen us lose to Porto after a thrilling second leg where we threatened to overturn a 4-0 first leg defeat.

It has got to the point where it is now an important part of Manchester United culture and history and I don't think the supporters would allow it to be any other way. Even in the disappointing latter days of David Moyes's recent reign, the supporters and team rejuvenated themselves to overturn a 2-0 first leg defeat and win 3-0 against Olympiacos in the Champions League.

That's how football should be played. Everyone played their part against Barcelona. Maradona was playing but a shadow of his usual self, despite how well Graeme Hogg played. Bryan scored again, as did Frank, to secure the turnaround in a frenzied atmosphere. The champagne was flowing afterwards yet because I was still not feeling great, despite the obvious jubilation, I didn't touch a drop. You could tell I wasn't feeling well as I would have been the first to have one!

Your debut is special as is winning trophies, and I had the honour of a testimonial, but I would have to say that the feeling I had in that game against Barcelona was the most incredible I've ever had at Old Trafford.

I'll stress again that every game is vitally important for United and you're aware of that as players but it's difficult as a sportsman to go from the high-intensity and high-velocity environment of the Barcelona game to going to the Hawthorns to play West Brom. It's not being unkind – you're bound to be on a comedown physically and emotionally. We lost 2-0 and maybe it was in these kind of games where the manager should have been earning his money.

You could never say an atmosphere is 'too' good but maybe that flat feeling afterwards infiltrated the confidence of the players. Theoretically, the win over Barcelona should have given us such a boost that we would take on the confidence, see our advantage in the single-point lead we had at the top of the division and see out the programme of fairly winnable games. There were tough trips to Everton and Nottingham Forest in there but we collected just ten points from our last ten league games. Eventually, we finished six points behind Liverpool, who won the title, but our late collapse saw us drop as low as fourth.

It wasn't just our league form that stuttered. Flat was the word I used there and it was the case against Juventus in the European semi-final. There wasn't the same kind of intensity or emotion. We got what we felt was a disappointing 1-1 result at Old Trafford to take into the second leg. Perhaps, when people talk about the benefit of having the second leg at home, it might have been better in this circumstance, but as professionals you have to deal with the hand you're dealt. We played okay in Italy but succumbed to a late goal – right at the end, in injury time, we conceded and were eliminated. It was a huge disappointment. Juventus were a strong side – European Cup finalists the year before – but the goal which decided it was so avoidable. Worse still, I felt culpable. I gave away the free kick, an annoying one because the player was going nowhere – I wasn't sure whether it was a free kick at all, but I was a bit annoyed either way. The free kick was delivered and Rossi was never going to miss.

I resolved to try and get forward afterwards and I went up and won a header to try and set up a chance – we didn't go anywhere. To say we were disappointed to have come away with such a result in Italy was a measure of how far we'd come as a team despite the bitter disappointment of how we finished in the league. Narrow margins. Juventus won in the European Cup Winners' Cup by defeating Porto, a team we felt we could have won against. Funnily enough, Porto's opponents in the semi-final were Aberdeen – on another day, we might well have been facing Alex Ferguson in the European Cup Winners' Cup Final of 1984.

Forest beat us on the last day to overtake us from fourth to third. To go from leading the table or being second most of the way to dropping off to fourth was disappointing. Were we jaded? I don't think so, not really. But this had happened for two seasons running. It wasn't just a one-off. The league is won over a season, not just a run-in.

Nonetheless, it doesn't affect how people look back on how we were in the 1980s – we were underachieving according to most people. Unless it's a trophy-winning season, people don't tend to look back on Manchester United's history favourably. Even Liverpool's recent years have been described as 'title challenging' – we came as close, if not closer, in our lean years, but they are described as underachievements. Such is the weight of expectation at Old Trafford. That's what makes United such a unique club, a different prospect altogether. Go anywhere in the world, mention Manchester United, and people will know. Not that our reputation did us any favours this season – and not only did we lose out in Europe to an Italian side, but we lost one of our better players to the country too, when Ray Wilkins left to join AC Milan.

I never had any similar temptations. I was happy in the north, it would have been far too much of a culture shock at the time. Ray was different – he was a star at Chelsea and fitted in really well in Milan. He was far more cosmopolitan than me – he loved it out there. The money would have been great but why would I have wanted to leave United? I wanted to win the league with them more than anything and I was still confident that it was only a matter of time.

9

'Show me a person who doesn't make mistakes and I'll show you a person who doesn't do anything.'

Leonard Ribino

THOUGH I'm very proud to say I played for my country, I think I've already hinted that I didn't always have the best of times in an England shirt. That said, it is a very special memory to have a very proud thing to say that I played in the last Home International tournament, and the 100th anniversary, at the end of the 1983/84 season. I grew up watching them and they would always be on television – I enjoyed watching them as a spectacle and I always thought about playing in them.

By the time I got around to doing so, something of the prestige had been taken away from the tournament. They'd tried to take it down the commercial avenue and it hadn't quite worked out, so it wasn't seen in the same light as it once was. Sadly, that did take some of the edge away from it for the players including myself. Still, that didn't stop the games being fiercely competed – with it being against club-mates or players you knew from other clubs, there was always that rivalry, but even then, there did seem to be something missing.

The competition had been finely poised. Northern Ireland had defeated Scotland with goals from Sammy McIlroy and Norman – Scotland then defeated Wales, and we got a win over Northern Ireland, meaning that our game with Wales was vital. This was the game that Sparky got the better of me, and for obvious reasons, that was one to forget for me.

The group really was up for grabs with every team having won and lost a game, but Wales and Northern Ireland drew 1-1, meaning that the winner of our game with Scotland at Hampden Park would win the tournament. No pressure.

The tournament had been structured throughout the season but our game with Scotland was on 26 May – at this time, we still went on the post-season tours, and the club were going to Hong Kong. Clubs were beginning to establish priority over international games and with the lucrative contracts on offer for these tours, I'm sure that the host countries had made it clear that they wanted to see proper United teams. You can see the logic otherwise it makes a mockery of it and it wouldn't be fair to the fans in those countries too.

We travelled with the United team to Hong Kong to play Bulova on 21 May, and straight after, we were on the plane. Myself, Ray Wilkins, who was still with the club at that point, Gary Bailey and Bryan Robson were absolutely shattered on that journey. The jet lag when we got back was ridiculous. It wasn't ideal preparation, but looking at what was to happen in my future, it was that trip to Hong Kong which sowed the seed for a future move.

My brief time there had gotten my interest and I wanted to see more – the vibrancy and safety of the environment and culture was very satisfying but the beauty of the place really caught me by surprise.

You hear about the density and the skyscrapers but there is a huge proportion of it that is a national park and it's glorious. Apparently you had to be a very skilled pilot to land at Hong Kong's old airport, Kai Tak, because as you're descending, you have to take a sharp right past the mountains and then between the buildings. You can see people having a cup of tea in their house from your aeroplane window – it's surreal. And the landing has to go perfectly too, or you'll end up in Victoria Harbour.

The opportunity to see all these different places really was a bonus to being a footballer and I tried to appreciate everything as much as I could. People will look at today's game and the obvious thing that most say or ask is about the money in the sport in the modern era. Yes, that's great, but for the time we were living in, we were also very lucky and had a fantastic lifestyle which I was very grateful for. I was playing football and being paid for doing so. We were given sportswear and clothing and being paid to market products. When I first broke in to the first team, Quicks in Manchester dealt with Ford cars which were club cars for United. I obviously didn't have one at first so I went to see the manager to ask for one – he said after ten first team games I could come and see him. Immediately after my tenth I went back as requested and got my car. It was a while after that until I picked up my first sportswear sponsorship and that was with Adidas who had a warehouse in Poynton. Rather than being paid, you could go and get boots, tracksuits and leisurewear. At that time I was highly delighted – I'd always wanted a pair of Adidas Gazelles and to get them for nothing, wow! It won't surprise many to know that I didn't have any major endorsements outside of that. I just saw them as perks of the job rather than financial opportunities.

We were being taken to the best places in the world and most of the time were staying in the best places – what is there not to like? Yes, there are minor grumbles like not being able to see as much as you might want to, but this was work. You were being paid to do these things. I did appreciate it at the time but even so, now, looking back, I do even more.

I was a little sad in a way to be returning to join up with England as the United lads were travelling to Australia and spending a fair amount of time there, so I admit to being more than just a bit envious of those lads as I'd always wanted to see the country. I wouldn't until much later in my life.

We may have been exhausted but it wasn't difficult at all to get psyched up to play against Scotland in Scotland, especially with something on the line. It is one of the oldest fixtures in football and was special to be a part of. Dad came up to watch it, too, having never been to see England play Scotland before. The atmosphere was good despite there being a restricted crowd due to building work.

As it stood, the winners would win the competition, but we drew 1-1, meaning that every team in the group finished on level points, and Northern Ireland won the whole thing courtesy of goal difference. The draw was a fair result but helped neither of us in the end.

It was strange after the game as every player went their own way. Arthur was playing for Scotland so I travelled back to Manchester with him in a taxi paid for by the FA. I was dropped off at The Tickled Trout Hotel in Preston where Karen picked me up. It had been difficult on her of course, we'd only been married for a short while and Ashley was only a few weeks old.

Hopes of a relaxing summer were out of the window, however, as the following week I was due to play with England again against the USSR at Wembley. My lapse that had allowed Hughes to score for Wales had been followed by blame for Scotland's goal too. Mark McGhee scored a header from around the edge of the box and as good as it looks, defenders and a goalkeeper will always get the blame if that happens and rightly so. I felt it was a little harsh for them to single me out as the one culpable when it was so far out, and all it did was add to my discomfort in a Three Lions shirt.

The Russia game wasn't any better. If there was one game in my career that I would have gladly grabbed a shovel, dug a hole and disappeared from the public eye, then that was the one. There was no disputing who was to blame – I went to trap the ball, but stood over it, tripped over and they ran through and scored. There was nothing I could do. The USSR won 2-0. It was painful to make that mistake – perhaps even more so because of the nature of it. Sometimes people say 'consistent and reliable' so much that it becomes a back-handed compliment but I was happy for people to describe my style as that. I didn't take risks even when I attacked, I made sensible decisions and was never too elaborate on the ball. So to make an error such as that was very frustrating, for it to come on the back of one that I didn't feel was my fault was more annoying because in a way, it becomes almost a vindication of that earlier comment.

When it's you against an opponent – like me against Sparky – there are two people in that situation. You can't always get the better of them but it doesn't stop the frustration you feel when they do get past you. The Russia one was a basic mistake that was an absolute fluke. It wasn't down to my decision-making.

I was annoyed, like I've said, but because it was such a fluke, I think most people who've played at a reasonably high level as a defender will understand where I'm coming from when I say I was more annoyed about the Hughes goal. However, it's obvious which one you'll get reminded of most often, isn't it? At the time, because of the coverage, the Russia one did feel a lot worse, but over time, I look back at the Hughes goal with more dissatisfaction.

I wasn't going to give up, even though I wasn't having the best of times, and I won't make any excuses for the errors.

They were things that happen on a football pitch and they've happened to hundreds, if not thousands, of other players. I had played 55 games for United that season, another five for England, and had been racking up the air miles since the end of the campaign but that wasn't going to stop me travelling on England's tour of South America which commenced almost immediately after the Russia game. At the age of 24 I was feeling like I could play 100 games a year.

In a contrast to how things had gone so far, the trip to South America was very enjoyable all around. I roomed with Kenny Sansom, who has since had his problems, but he was very good to be around. He was a lot louder and more vociferous than myself but that was good in a way, for me.

The highlight of that time was without doubt the win over Brazil, which everyone remembers to this day for the fabulous goal by John Barnes. I had grown up watching Brazil and seeing the Maracana so to go there and actually win was incredible. Like my first impression of Wembley, though, this famous stadium was a little underwhelming – it was only around a quarter full with 56,000, a good crowd anywhere else but not there.

The pitch wasn't great either, but neither of those things could detract from what a marvellous achievement it was. I swapped shirts with Tato, their number 11. I put the shirt on and the press were all over me asking to take pictures. Happier times than a week before, that's for sure. Unlike the United tours I'd been on, we got a real opportunity to see some of the country, to have a stroll on the Copacabana beach and see the statue of Christ the Redeemer, which helped to forge a really fond memory of the country.

From then it was on to Uruguay which seemed to resemble 1950s North America, with its Dodge cars. It was like stepping into the day before yesterday, in a way. The result wasn't the greatest there, as we lost, but we got a decent result against Chile with a goalless draw in the last game.

Despite the pressures I'd played every minute of my eight England games so far and, significantly, the three on the tour which had followed the Russia mistake. I was grateful to England manager Bobby Robson for the faith he showed though I think I would have preferred it more if there was a little more talking or guidance, or personal reassurance. It wasn't always clear what the defender's role was, whether we should sit or help the attackers. Bobby was obviously a very successful manager and must have felt at the time that less was more but I think in my case, less was not enough. Regardless, I played as well for England as I ever did in those three tour games so I was happy with my own response.

Returning to England, I took the responsibility of staying home and helping Karen where I could, and preparing for the new season as close to Manchester as I was. And there was a lot of activity at the club – Ron Atkinson had been under a bit of pressure after another late-season collapse and sought to address that with major moves for Jesper Olsen, Gordon Strachan, and Alan Brazil.

I hadn't seen much of Jesper but knew of his reputation and we were well aware of the qualities of the Scottish duo – I thought all three were brilliant signings and just what we needed. Perhaps we still could have done with that goalkeeper but United had always concentrated on the scoring of goals rather than keeping them out and these were certainly signings that were going to help us do that. In Jesper, particularly, we had addressed that left side problem that had existed for a few years.

Quite how the team would shape up with Gordon and Alan, I wasn't completely sure, but with almost 200 appearances at the club, I was more or less the established name in front of Giddy at right-back. Or so I thought, anyway. My relationship with Ron, or at least my perception of what he thought of me, was such that I felt that if anyone was going to get dropped, it would be me. Tactical shifts were pretty rare so if you were dropped you knew it would more than likely be because you weren't playing well, as simple as that, and as well as I thought I had done over the last two years, sometimes I felt it was more of a case that I just needed to give Ron an excuse to drop me and he'd have no qualms in doing so.

It's gone down in folklore now about the drinking culture at the club and after spending so much time pondering over just what it was that caused our inconsistency it's not only the right time to mention this but it would probably be ignorant not to.

Ron once said, 'Never trust a player who doesn't drink.' I'll admit that I indulged, though I tried to do it at the right times. Whenever there was an arrangement in the team to go out, I'd join in. If there was a meal, I'd be there, and if there was somewhere else to go after the meal, then I'd be there too, and have a good time and go home as late as anybody. I'd try and limit it to weekends – I had my moments, at certain times, but I never went stupid. I felt I always had the self-discipline to say no, and still felt as much a part of the team as I did before.

Perhaps it was easier for me because I had to travel out of Manchester to get home and those who lived closer together might have found it harder to separate. It is left to others to speculate who was part of the group who socialised more and whether or not that group were looked upon more favourably by Ron. Did I think it went on too much? Well, it wasn't down to me, and in fairness if it was a problem, then it was a problem in football, not just United.

It's important to acknowledge that just because there was a drinking habit and a culture, it didn't mean there was a drinking problem per se. But I suppose it's natural to wonder what might have been if Ron had had more discipline and cut it out in the way that Sir Alex tried to do later. Bryan Robson and Norman Whiteside were absolutely fantastic players. Bryan was captain of his club and country, he carried the team so many times and scored so many important goals. Norman was a colossal player for us too. They both got us out of so many holes. If you were to look at it logically and ask whether without the drink, could we and they have achieved more and done better, you would have to say yes, but then it's hard to fathom just how good they might have been because they were, for me at least, world-class players who were vital to our team as they were.

Easy as it is to point out the drinking culture as a problem, the fact that it existed at all the top clubs meant that nobody had an advantage over the others. Of course, without the drink, we'd have all played better, but at the end of any given game if you were to start pointing the finger at someone and wondering if they'd done their jobs then Norman and Bryan would always be safe. I don't think you could ever do that at any United player but those two especially could never be questioned. If I could choose any team-mates from my career to have beside me in the trenches those would be the top ones I'd select.

There were some unbelievable stories I've heard about what happened at Liverpool – none I can print! – but their best trait was consistency. Perhaps it would have been a sign of good management to see the stop of it as a potential advantage but at the time we didn't feel like it put us at a disadvantage.

Going into the new season, it was still Norman and Bryan who would be our main men despite the new signings we'd got in. Those new men were supposed to help us get that consistency going and in a way they did but not quite as we wanted – we got a run of four straight draws at the start of the 1984/85 season, which at least was consistent in a way! Our last game before the international break was against Newcastle and we gave them a thumping, 5-0, with Jesper and Gordon on the scoresheet.

My penultimate England cap came in September 1984 against the tough East Germany side who always had a reputation of being tough to beat. Bryan scored the winner in a 1-0 scoreline and I had a hand in the goal.

Back in Manchester, the rest of our September went swimmingly. As I've said at an earlier point, draws can be good for momentum if you turn them into wins and that's what we did – knocking a few goals past Burnley in the League Cup, getting through against Hungarian opponents Rabas in the UEFA Cup, and picking up good wins at Coventry and West Brom. Liverpool came to Old Trafford in the month and we got a good draw against them, with Strachan scoring a penalty. The little Scot had really taken to life at Old Trafford and settled in really well. Sadly, my season wasn't going quite as swimmingly – although I was playing okay, I picked up a calf injury in mid-October which ruled me out for a few weeks. I was actually playing for England against Finland when I picked it up. I came off at half-time and never played for my country again.

I missed the European tie with Dutch team PSV – decided by another Strachan spot-kick in Manchester – but was back in the side for the next round tie against Dundee United. That was one heck of a pair of games. They really came at us at Old Trafford and although we were ahead 2-1, Paul Sturrock scored to get them a draw and, perhaps just as important, two away goals. It made our task at Tannadice doubly difficult but we still went into the second leg confident. We went up to Scotland and stayed at St Andrews – another lovely place.

They proved to be just as resilient opponents at home as they had been in Manchester, never saying die – we took an early lead through Mark Hughes, they equalised. We got an advantage just before half-time through an own goal but they got level again early in the second. It was a proper end to end battle and a really tough one for me playing at centre-half. Arnold Muhren scored with just about a quarter of an hour left and then they threw the kitchen sink at us. I remember being stood on the edge of the box and having to clear dozens of balls pumped into the box. Big Gordon McQueen had one of the games of his life. The atmosphere was fantastic and I think people expected that we would get beat in the second leg.

We took that confidence into the next game and got a comprehensive 3-0 win over QPR. Being rivals for a first team position, I suppose it was rare to see me and Giddy playing together, let alone scoring in the same game, but we did so here, and Alan Brazil got the other. I remember my goal clearly – I played a one-two with Alan at the edge of the box and side-footed it in to the net. One particular point of satisfaction to take from that goal is that for the next few weeks it was shown on the opening montage of *Match of the Day*.

A couple of days after that game we were invited to play in a friendly for another legend – but instead of this being a football legend, like George Best or Johan Cruyff, this game was for a cricket legend, Ian Botham, up at Scunthorpe.

I spoke to Ian for a while in the bar afterwards and he was lovely – he said a few nice things about me too which was pleasing to hear. The game was a proper testimonial, with a 5-5 scoreline. Ian was one of those you could tell wanted to be a footballer. There aren't many who've made the crossover – I remember Arnie Sidebottom playing cricket and football and everyone says Phil Neville would have made a great cricketer too. In recent years Brian Lara and Usain Bolt have both intimated an interest in playing football, too.

I was a bit starstruck meeting Ian, I must confess. Being in Manchester you might have thought we would often bump into personalities from either the sporting or celebrity world but being a relatively private person it didn't happen too often to me. Once, Simply Red came into the changing room before a game, with Mick Hucknall being a United supporter. Karen and I are big fans of the band and Mick in particular. If I'd have been in my right mind, in any other situation, I would have loved nothing more than to go and shake his hand and probably do something stupid like bow down in front of him. But I was doing my pre-match thing of zoning out and completely allowed the moment to pass me by. I've regretted that ever since.

It was a mixed Christmas for us. The QPR result had put us in third place, keeping touch with Everton at the top, but we then won one and lost one for six league games in a row, which put us eight points behind in the middle of January. The first of those defeats was a 2-1 loss at Stoke City on Boxing Day, which was my 200th appearance for the club. To be completely honest I didn't really pay much attention to these landmarks, as fantastic, humbling and memorable as they are, at the time. I would tend to notice birthdays more – being away on my 21st birthday for example. When I became a teacher, we went back to school after the holidays on my 40th birthday – 1 September – it's never normally that early. The exact same thing happened on my 50th. You could not make it up!

The turn of the year in 1985 saw us get a good opportunity to get revenge on Bournemouth as we were drawn against them in the FA Cup. Those comments they had made were fresh in the mind and concentration was never going to be an issue. Perhaps everyone was wanting to see a repeat upset but they didn't get it – Strachan, McQueen and Stapleton made comfortable work of them with goals in a 3-0 win.

It was revenge we were looking for in the next round too – Coventry defeated us at Old Trafford and our very next game was the same side at the same venue. A 2-1 win put us in to the fifth round but in the defeat to Coventry I'd picked up another injury and was out for around a month. John came in at right-back and kept his position when I was fit again – when I got back in the team, I was in midfield, and played in that role for a few games as we picked up decent results in victories over Arsenal and West Ham and a draw against Everton.

Around this time, we faced Videoton of Hungary in the UEFA Cup. After winning the first leg 1-0 at Old Trafford we travelled for the second leg and it was largely one to forget for all reasons. We had a few problems in the preparation with our pre-match meal. We'd take some things with us, the odd chocolate bar and things like that. A few years previous Alf Ramsey had taken boxes of food that his England players were familiar with to the World Cup in Mexico and that appeared to offend the hosts, who felt their food was more than acceptable. You can see both sides. Anyway, in Hungary, we'd taken the chocolate bars for a quick post-meal energy boost. We asked for them afterwards and they misunderstood, bringing out a jug of chocolate milk that they had melted down from our bars. Then we explained and so they brought their own chocolate bars. Norman took a bite of one and a maggot started crawling out of it! Yuck. Not the best start.

The match didn't go well at all. We conceded a goal we probably shouldn't have and it went all the way to penalties. It was a horrible, horrible night and felt like we'd never win. Arthur missed the decisive penalty but that didn't really matter because as a team we should have done better. I'd be the last to criticise anyone who missed a penalty because I would never have wanted to take one. You'd find me last in the queue, behind the goalkeeper even, because it was not my thing at all. At St Mary's School we had a competition at Ewood Park to take penalties and I missed one at each end. I don';t think I ever recovered from that feeling. 'You should always score a penalty,' everyone says, but someone always misses. No, not for me. As disappointed as we were to lose, we were relieved and happy to be travelling away from Hungary.

I was out of the team again after this but this time I was dropped. Giddy was playing well at right-back and our midfield was now fully fit. That meant I missed some great games with Liverpool and I was so upset to have missed them. We won at Anfield in the league and then had two great matches with them in the semi-final of the FA Cup, overcoming them in the replay thanks to a Hughes goal. I'm not unreasonable, if a team is playing well, sometimes you don't make changes, and it was up to me to force my way back in. United had cut the gap from eight points to four on Everton but had played two games more at the start of April – perhaps the distraction of the semi-final was too much as United didn't win for four league games, putting them nine points behind Everton at the top and the Toffees had three games in hand. We had no chance of catching them. We were in second place as we finished our league programme but loads of teams around us had games in hand and we ended up in fourth.

Thoughts turned to the FA Cup and we'd proven we could match anyone on their day. In my first absence from the team, we'd been battered 5-0 at Goodison Park, and Everton had knocked us out of the League Cup, but even though they were nailed on to win the league, we were still confident of getting the right result. My immediate concern, though, was to try and get back in to the team. And if not the team, try and make a convincing argument for myself to be considered as the substitute. Hard to imagine, but there was still only one sub in those days. Bryan was missing from the team in the build-up to the final and I was surprised to get the nod in the number seven shirt in his absence but there was no way I was going to be wearing his shirt on FA Cup Final day.

When it got down to the last training session before the final I was more or less aware it was down to me or Alan Brazil who would get the nod as substitute. On Friday afternoon, Ron came over to me and told me that I'd be sub. I know that Alan was told some time later and I kept my news to myself – I think he was told on the coach that he wouldn't be included and he took it as a massive, massive disappointment.

It put it into some perspective for me that I was grateful to at least be in the squad but it was still a huge disappointment given the fact I'd started in the last final. Everyone wants to be in the starting 11 in a final. You don't wish ill of your team-mates but you're hoping to get on as early as the first minute. I didn't, and neither manager appeared ready to make a change as the game remained very tense and closely fought. Then Kevin Moran was sent off with 12 minutes left. Still, Ron made only a tactical shift and didn't bring me on – it wasn't until the full-time whistle with the score at 0-0, and Arthur struggling with an injury, that I was brought on at left-back.

I'd missed the majority of the game but I was delighted to be on the field when Norman struck that beautiful goal in the second period of extra time that decided things. He did that day in and day out in training – the move to cut inside and swing the left foot of his. I could watch it again and again – a goalkeeper of Neville Southall's class was well beaten and he was never going to get there. He knew where it was going but simply had no chance.

For the club it was a great day. With all the talk about Liverpool in the 1970s and 80s people forget just how good that Everton team was and who knows what they could have done in the European Cup. We'd done very well to beat them, that's for definite. Not that we were fortunate or undeserving. I thought we were the better team on the day and I later found out we were the first team to win the FA Cup where every single player had won international caps – and, I was delighted to be one of a select group of players (most of them I was on the pitch with) to have won two FA Cup medals with Manchester United.

I took part in the celebrations afterwards and it was great to win a second FA Cup but it didn't feel the same as the first time if I'm being honest. The spark wasn't quite the same for me as I'd been marginalised from the squad for the last few weeks and I couldn't just forget that disappointment. The injuries had disrupted my season and it had been difficult to recover my best form playing in different positions when I was recalled. Even though I would be the first to admit it was not my best year, I was still surprised by the line of questioning I received when faced with the *Match of the Day* cameras afterwards. 'So Mike, a pleasing day after what must have been a disappointing season for you personally,' said Jimmy Hill. 'Thanks for that, Jimmy!' I replied. Great boost of confidence!

I know it's selfish but it did feel like something was missing. I wonder how other players feel in the same situation. I'd had a dip in form and in that respect I couldn't really argue with Ron's decision but I did feel a little resentment towards him because of it, though I hasten to add that our indifferent relationship to that point was very much the catalyst.

I can't imagine I felt as bad as Kevin Moran, though. He was despondent, distraught. At the time we all thought he should have only got a yellow and were so surprised. As a result of the red card he wasn't allowed to go up the stairs and collect his medal at the end. We eventually got him to enjoy himself in the party afterwards but how much of that was forced, I wasn't sure. It had been a tough season for him as he had spent ten weeks injured and he didn't deserve it to end like that.

Events to follow meant that neither Everton nor ourselves would be able to follow our respective successes with trying to prove ourselves in Europe, but it did at least mean that we would be facing Howard Kendall's side at Wembley again in August.

10

False Dawns

A FEW days after winning the FA Cup, we were on another of those post-season tours, this time to Trinidad. It was another place we hadn't been to but just like the previous year, we were flying out with another English team – this time Southampton – to play in front of local supporters.

On the flight over, Kevin Moran was given the good news via a message back in Manchester that he would receive his medal for winning the FA Cup after all. Perhaps, in fairness to the FA, Kevin had set an unwanted record by becoming the first man sent off in the final so it was unprecedented territory they were heading into by making a decision.

It was unprecedented territory for us, too, in Trinidad. It wasn't a typical place to go to and not exactly known for its football roots. I didn't mind the journeys and in fact the opportunity to see these new places is something I cherished but this was probably the first time that I felt that playing football after such a long, hard season was the last thing I wanted to do, especially in these ultimately meaningless friendlies. That was the feeling among the players too – it was pretty flat. Maybe that had something to do with our surroundings, the

Caribbean is so laid back and relaxed and I'm not sure that we felt we could relax when there were games to play.

That was a factor as we lost 1-0 to Southampton and a George Lawrence goal. A couple of days later we faced a local select 11 in a game we won in incredible heat. Before one of the games, a gimmick had been arranged where a parachutist would come in and 'deliver' the match ball. I think he actually hit the stand on the way down and got injured – he certainly didn't do what he was supposed to. It was completely bizarre from start to finish.

It would have been nice if the club had just taken us away for a few days to relax after another tough season but I suppose, with the commercial pull that Manchester United have, it was never going to be that simple. Taking the rough with the smooth – it was just part and parcel of what we'd become accustomed to. I feel sorry for the players and supporters alike in these far away destination tours. We're all human and we get tired. Of course we appreciate the opportunities but the players aren't in the best of condition to put on their finest performances, whether it's at the beginning or end of a season.

We did have a good time when we could, after we settled. The first hotel we got to was so disappointing nobody even unpacked their bags. We were told we couldn't travel overnight because of bandits in the hills so we had to leave early in the morning in a minibus. It wasn't the greatest of trips.

The lack of discipline that Ron had instilled in the team meant that we all got a little carried away with indulging and I include myself in that. Things are great when everything is going well – and after the FA Cup win, that's how it all seemed to be – but there comes a point where you have to maintain some control. Maybe the events of the next 16 months or so proved that the line between discipline and enjoyment had just become a little blurry for the manager.

Yes, we'd be told to be at places at a certain time, so it was never unorganised as such, but what I mean is that normally there is a time and a place for letting your hair down. We'd all begun to do that but then there was nobody to rein us in but ourselves. At the end of a season, you don't see the damage in it because it's part of the fun and seems like the right time, but moving forward, maybe it did play a part in what was to happen. The players had a choice and a responsibility too and they took advantage of the freedom that was given. But maybe that's the point.

I go back to the culture at the time and there must have been a fine line between instilling that discipline and maintaining consistency and what we were. Because I'm sure we had the ability. Do you blame the players for that? Well partly yes, but the manager ought to take some of the responsibility. It may sound like I'm being overly critical of Ron and making him solely responsible for our failure to fulfil our potential and I have to cut back a little and reinforce the fact that it was part of the culture in football. Perhaps Ron's reign is unfairly viewed because of what his successor did and it's easy to say anything with the benefit of hindsight. One thing I would never shirk away from saying is that the players were at least equally responsible for our supposed under-performance in the 1980s.

The plus point of our actions was that we were creating a bonding and a togetherness which we wouldn't have otherwise had and perhaps that's what Ron was going for. The argument is whether that went too far but certainly at the time our manager could say his management style was justified because it was bringing some success.

And I have to be fair to Ron again and say that after a successful European Cup Winners' Cup run in 1984, there's no telling what we might have done with that experience under our belt, but he was unable to do that because of events elsewhere.

The Heysel disaster which happened prior to the 1985 European Cup Final between Juventus and Liverpool had seen 39 supporters lose their lives and, consequently, all English clubs were banned from participating in European competition. While the decision was being taken, this meant for English clubs travelling to even play friendlies abroad, the safer choice for everyone was for us to have a pre-season at home, which was a rare schedule indeed. Cambridge, Hereford, and Bristol City were our opponents before a game against Bradford City to attempt to raise money to help after their own disaster – the fire at their home ground at Valley Parade which resulted in 56 lives lost. I'd actually played for United's reserves at Bradford the week before the fire.

On the whole, football grounds had been pretty safe – there were isolated incidents, and of course the hooligan problems, but it was absolutely horrid to see what happened in Heysel. As tragic as the events were, I felt the punishments on English clubs were incredibly harsh. For us to not even have any involvement in anything that happened and lose our opportunity to play in the Cup Winners' Cup was very disappointing. At the time, we had no way of knowing if we would ever get the opportunity to play in Europe again. It wasn't that we were having a go at Liverpool or blaming anyone, it was just us feeling so very disappointed. The ban, as it was, lasted around five years, which meant I wouldn't play in Europe again.

Our pre-season programme complete, we faced Everton in the Charity Shield. I was brought off at half-time for Remi Moses with Ron's reasoning being, 'It's a chance to give your mate a game.' It seemed like an excuse rather than a reason. We lost 2-0.

I was beginning to feel a little out of place and I wasn't very comfortable with it. Every professional wants to be playing, don't they? I accept that not everyone can. There's only 11 players after all. But I felt I was now being used as a makeshift player to fill in when someone else was available – I'd suffered one dip in form and was instantly dropped and then asked to fill in elsewhere.

I played as well as I could to try and force my way back into the reckoning but it was admittedly a little difficult to do when I always had at the back of my mind that I was never the manager's preference anyway. I did begin to wonder if it was personal, or if I was a bad player. I didn't rock the boat – admittedly, I wasn't exactly a superstar, but I felt I was applying myself well.

My short-term concern wasn't about playing in Europe but playing at all. I started the season on the bench with my appearances looking like they would come in midfield when John Gidman suffered an injury in our second league game at Ipswich. I'd had my own concerns about my place but I certainly didn't wish ill on John or any of my team-mates. John was 31 and I was almost 26 – approaching my peak, I was determined to put the disappointment of my last year behind me and establish myself once more. We'd won both of our opening fixtures and I was coming in at my natural position so I was confident that I would be able to hit the ground running. I don't know if I would say it's easier to come into a winning team. I suppose it is, but you still have to make sure that your performance levels match it, because United isn't normally a club that carries passengers.

I wouldn't call Peter Barnes a passenger by a long chalk but he had travelled with us as a guest on our pre-season of 1984 and in August 1985 he signed for the club permanently. He broke on to the scene around the same time as Gordon Hill in the mid-1970s and now nearly at the end of his career, he was another player who was brought in to do a job for a short period of time rather than a long-term signing.

The first ten league matches of the 1985/86 season have gone down in United folklore. For the football that we played I would have to say that short period was the best I ever felt in the United team. The supporters loved it and I'm sure I can speak for the players when I say we did too. At times I would just admire the way my team-mates were playing. We got fantastic results at Ipswich and Arsenal and then we won at Forest, too. In that game at the City Ground there was a passage of play where Gary Bailey made a save, passed it to me, and I helped the ball on. From then on we put together a move that I'm not even sure we scored from but was incredible to watch. For a second, I lost myself, and felt like a supporter in the stand, marvelling at what I'd seen my colleagues do. Peter scored his first goal, a debut goal in a 3-1 win on that day. It was unbelievable. The confidence was really beginning to rub off on us all and we were all raising our own games as a consequence.

For everything I've said that may appear negative about the manager one thing I have to say is that under Ron Atkinson, Manchester United were always going to play good football. Whether that was a reflection of the manager and the freeness he encouraged, I don't know.

It's one thing playing good football, it's another putting goals away, and we were doing both. Four on the first day against Aston Villa, three at Forest, then three in consecutive games against Newcastle, Oxford, and Manchester City. We felt unbeatable. I scored at City which topped it all off for me! At Maine Road, we'd taken an early lead through Bryan and then Arthur scored a great goal. I can't remember why I'd decided to go up but Alex Williams in the City goal left a huge gap to the right-hand side. There was an area between his left hand and the post – I toe-poked the ball past him and into the corner. My celebration was crazy, a forward roll and a jump in the air. I didn't know what to do. It was pure excitement. Those ten wins were concluded with a huge 5-1 win at West Brom and then a 1-0 victory over Southampton.

It was without a shadow of a doubt the best football I've ever partaken in because it was so attacking and brought so many goals. My memories of great football start with Brazil in 1970 and then the latter days of Tommy Docherty's reign at United. That was what I considered the best football I'd seen but for that ten-game period at the start of 1985/86 I'd like to think we played as well as any United side could and it was a true privilege as a player to be a part of. Even as a defender it was important for me that good football had an end product. Brazil could point to success in the World Cup and United won the FA Cup in 1977. This technically was our FA Cup-winning side too. Perhaps if we'd have won the ten games prior to the FA Cup Final rather than the ten games after that team may have been looked upon differently.

I suppose that kind of opinion enters into the debate of what was the best ever team and what style of football has been the best. That is a matter of opinion but I do find it interesting when people talk about how teams would have done in certain eras. I think that it's natural that most people would conclude that today's teams would struggle – or, perhaps I ought to say, they'd have to find a different way to approach the game – on pitches from the 1970s and 80s, while those great early teams might even be far better on today's pitches. One thing that did interest me was that there was a shift in attitudes and the facilities in South America. A lot of great playing surfaces were installed and players were actually suffering because of it – so some clubs actually churned the surfaces, so that it caused bobbles.

It's a question that can never be answered but it does bring to mind a friendly played at the end of the 1987/88 season when we hosted AC Milan. The pitch wasn't in great shape and the likes of Gullit simply adjusted their style to volleying the ball around the pitch. It was marvellously done even though it was against us!

In the early autumn of 1985, though, we were playing football that was on a par with any of the great teams and it was a sign of how well we were doing that every single outfield player including myself was getting involved in the forward play often and scoring, too. We were scoring and not giving many goals away. It was the right sort of momentum rather than irresponsible – we were controlled and felt unbeatable.

With ten straight wins we were obviously top but the nine-point lead we had established was a sign of how well we'd done. People always mention the ten but don't always say that we went 15 unbeaten, winning three of those next five games too. Two of those five games were consecutive games against Liverpool at Old Trafford and Chelsea, who had won every home game, at Stamford Bridge. We drew in the first and won the second, and these felt like hugely significant results at the time. To illustrate the point about how well we'd done, after those 15 games we'd scored 35 goals and conceded just six. Mark Hughes had scored ten goals, with Robson, Strachan and Olsen getting a few too.

None of the players were counting any chickens but we knew we were building a formidable advantage. If it's fair to say that what followed was a surprise, the extent to which everything changed at Old Trafford over the next 12 months could probably not have been predicted by Nostradamus himself.

11

The Tough Winter

IT seems crazy to say and is admittedly with the benefit of hindsight but there are, sometimes, negative repercussions of things going a little too well. I'd like to think that the players had suffered enough in recent seasons to know that complacency was not going to be an issue.

I'll never be one to blow up my own importance so much as to say our dramatic loss of form was down to my absence from the team but what I think can be taken from the events of the early winter of 1985 was that perhaps Ron Atkinson learned the pitfalls of changing a winning team. After winning in the League Cup against West Ham, I was out of the team, with John Gidman selected again after his recovery from injury.

Giddy's return to the side coincided with a 1-0 defeat at Sheffield Wednesday. Wednesday had been a bit of a bogey side for us and all runs have to end – but when we failed to score at home to Tottenham in a draw and then fell to a 3-0 defeat at Leicester City, the good times were certainly over and the hard work was beginning. We lost at Anfield in the League Cup – a result that normally wouldn't be that much of a surprise but we hadn't lost there since 1980. After going so long unbeaten, the club went a month without a win.

After everything had seemed so positive, my memory of that time at Manchester United is simply 'grey'. It was like a large cloud had just appeared over us and there was no way of shifting it. Ron was faced with a situation he hadn't had before – we'd always been there or thereabouts but never so far in front of the pack that we were overwhelming favourites. Yes, we had a couple of injuries, but you can ask any player and I'm sure they'll say the same. I can't put my finger on why our form dropped so spectacularly and that's where I have some sympathy with Ron, because it was such an unusual situation. Ultimately, our collapse was something that marked the beginning of the end. You might even say that our early season heights had made expectations a little too unrealistic – but Ron had spent a lot of money and now the vultures were beginning to circle. Consecutive defeats to Arsenal and Everton over the Christmas period saw our commanding lead cut to just four points at the end of Boxing Day.

Ron must have felt that defensively we needed changes and finally went with the move to sign Chris Turner as a goalkeeper to replace Gary Bailey, although the two seemed to share the position for a couple of months before Chris became the established number one. You can see the logic behind the move, as I would agree that we needed a top-class goalkeeper. Chris was a solid, dependable stopper, but was more of a sideways step than the significant improvement we had hoped for. While you could certainly see what Ron was doing and why he was doing it, it could be argued that it was either too late or simply the wrong time to make those calls, and the inconsistent selection in defence did more harm than good.

I had become the forgotten man for a while with some of the players sometimes coming to me and sympathising with my situation. They were all encouraging of me when I was selected for our FA Cup third round tie with Rochdale, but after that, I was out of the side for another month. More than being substituted, the situation of being used as a squad player drafted in to rest others as Rochdale was a game we should easily win was one of the biggest professional insults I could have gotten from Ron, and my dissatisfaction was at its peak.

Players are inherently selfish and I'm no different. I knew now I was not Ron's first choice and when he signed John Sivebaek it would have been easy for me to just give up. I'd been dropped when I was playing well and instead of putting me back in when things weren't going great for the team, Ron's solution was to spend. This may sound bad and unprofessional but at the time of the signing of Sivebaek I was almost looking at it from the point of view that Ron probably wasn't going to be manager for much longer because he was making one or two hasty calls. He wasn't dealing with the pressure and his only reaction was to spend.

I wouldn't say he 'lost' the dressing room and I was certainly not going to be satisfied by seeing my club lose even if I wasn't in the team but it would be very fair to say I was losing what faith I did have in his ability to get us back to where we were. As players, you look to what you can do to turn it around. For me, what could I do apart from get on with my job? If you can't do anything or feel unable then you look to the manager for guidance. The signings of Turner and Sivebaek, as well as Colin Gibson, seemed to suggest he didn't have faith in the team, which would naturally provoke a lack of confidence. Worse still, although they were good professionals, they were hardly the kind of landmark signings that would give the entire place a lift.

In January, it was rumoured that Mark Hughes had agreed a deal to sign for Barcelona. Ron's pre-emptive strike was to bring in Peter Davenport and Terry Gibson. He was throwing money at a problem and not making it any better. All the lads were great blokes, I roomed with Terry for a while, and I don't really like saying it but you have to be brutally honest and say that the players Ron was bringing in were just not what you would describe as Manchester United players. They could all certainly do a job and as squad players may well have been perceived a lot more generously over time but they were marked men, brought in to turn the club's fortunes around and hopefully secure that league title that we all desperately wanted. In a sense, it was almost as unfair to those who came in as those who were there.

I think if you were to look at it and consider that Ron had been at the club for a good few years, the fact that he made so many changes in such a short space of time was probably an indication of the pressure he was under. Panic buys, if you want to call them that. The players are only human too and they can tell if the manager is under pressure, certainly for those of us who were more senior and experienced. You learn more about the character of people when times are hard.

After the turn of the year we were really struggling. Having signed John Sivebaek, Ron understandably had to back his judgement and play him. That meant more time in the reserves for me, although if the first team were playing on a Sunday, I'd still travel with them.

I was back in the starting 11 for our FA Cup defeat to West Ham and then part of the travelling squad for a friendly in Israel to play Maccabi Haifa. It was an absurd time to have a friendly so far away particularly with the political climate. The trip to Israel was probably just as memorable for the prank we pulled on Mick Brown. We were staying within the hotel compound for security reasons. One of the mornings we were out on the beach doing a bit of running and working on our fitness when we came across this giant turtle which had been washed up on the beach – well, it was a big turtle, probably not a giant but bigger than anything certainly I'd seen before. Gary Bailey, Lee

Martin, and myself decided we were going to take the turtle into the hotel.

That night we were helped by a local to escape the hotel perimeters (which involved climbing over a barbed wire fence) who drove us to the beach. We were going to drive it back but for some reason that escapes me now, we couldn't put it in the car. Anyway, we carried it back and lifted it over the fence – we'd taken hotel bedsheets to wrap it in. There was a putrid smell coming from it, something seemed to be oozing. We hadn't actually decided what we were going to do with it but then we agreed – Mick Brown's bedroom. We went to reception and got his room key as he was still down having his evening meal. We took the turtle up into Mick's room and went into the bathroom, put it in the bath and ran a bit of water. We put the room flowers on the turtle's back, made a hasty exit and went into Gordon Strachan's room where a couple of the lads were playing cards.

We were waiting for a reaction but what greeted us first was the smell – it absolutely reeked, and everyone on the floor must have been able to smell it. In the end it got so bad we had to go and take the turtle out before Mick came back. He might not even know about it to this day. We managed to smuggle it out of reception where the local who had helped us took it away. I think he said he was going to take the shell off but we never knew what became of it.

I did try and join in the fun where I could – cutting the ties, emptying toothpaste, soaking a player's bed, things like that. It sounds crazy for professional sportsmen to be doing things like that. I was probably a victim of them many times without even knowing.

Again, it was good to go and see a beautiful country even if this was more of a brief tour. The only downside was that now having a young family, I really wish that Karen could have been there, and perhaps that feeling was intensified by the feeling around the club.

We were attempting to raise spirits internally but the line-up for the friendly – Bailey, Sivebaek, Albiston, Duxbury, McGrath, Higgins, Colin Gibson, Strachan, Stapleton, Terry Gibson and Barnes – showed the changes that were taking place.

Higgins was Mark Higgins. He'd been a steady club player at Everton, another reliable professional, but a very strange signing. He had retired due to injury in May 1984 but Everton kept his registration. Ron signed him in December 1985 for £60,000. I was really pleased as a fellow professional that Mark went on to play around 100 more times in the league for Bury and Stoke but I think it was too much of an ask for him to do what United and Ron needed him to. And, as another defender, it was yet another kick in the teeth for me. Had Sivebaek or Higgins been so outstanding that I could only hold my hands up and concede that a better player had my place then fair enough. But that wasn't the case, I felt I was certainly as good as them. In a weird way, that almost strengthened my resolve to remain at the club and see it through. It was like a storm.

My best form, personally, had been in the 1982/83 season but 1985/86 had seen the best, then the worst, times I'd experienced at Old Trafford. By the end of February we had been overtaken at the top of the table and by the middle of March we were down to third. From February until the end of the season we didn't win consecutive games. That can be put down to anything you like although the most likely reason is simply the number of changes that were made.

Change might have been on the cards for me too as I received the crushing blow that Ron had accepted an offer from Everton for me. Gary Stevens, their right-back, had got injured, so Howard Kendall made a £250,000 bid for me. I can remember the lads saying to me that they were shocked that the club had accepted an offer so low. It never got so far as me having to turn Everton down, though, because I said in no uncertain terms that I would not leave United. I don't know if that was stubbornness on my part or if a part of me believed that the Atkinson era would soon be over, so all I had to do was wait.

At Manchester United you're always feeling the pressure anyway but there was such a strange atmosphere. I can only speak for myself but I wouldn't have been surprised if there were others feeling the same way, that others were upset with the number of players who had come in. I felt that going to Israel when I was barely playing for the first team was like I was being used, in a way, particularly after the Rochdale game.

I was back in the squad fairly regularly as the season drew to a close but that was a bit like shutting the stable door after the horse has bolted. Despite our run of poor form we had achieved draws at Liverpool and against Everton, but after consecutive defeats at Old Trafford to Chelsea and Sheffield Wednesday in the space of four days in mid-April, the title was essentially out of reach. We were five points behind the Merseyside clubs who both had games in hand over us.

We were unbeaten in our last four fixtures but West Ham won some of their matches in hand to overtake us. We finished a season which had started with such promise in fourth position. Our final day was a disappointing draw at Watford, with Sparky scoring to give us all a reminder of what we'd be missing when he joined Barcelona.

To be blunt, I would have been happy to see a change in manager at this point. It's never nice to see someone lose their job but the calamitous way we had played in the second half of the season as well as the gambles that hadn't come off meant that Ron was on the brink.

I don't think he came with us on our post-season tour to the Far East (if he did, I certainly didn't see him!) which was very strange. Mick Brown was in charge of us for the trip. Our first game was in Singapore and I scored – it was great to be out there and the weather was great. It was a strange time to visit as there was a huge political debate about potentially banning chewing gum. It was a very sterile atmosphere, if that's the right word. Maybe they were ahead of their time, with the banning of public smoking too. Being told you couldn't do this or couldn't do that was a bit odd, though.

We played further matches in Bangkok and then Hong Kong to close the tour. Returning to Hong Kong was great, and as meaningless as those friendlies were, the tour was a nice lift of spirits to close off what had been an otherwise disappointing campaign.

12

'A man is judged by his deeds, not his words.'

Anon

I WAS a little surprised to report back to first team training with Ron Atkinson still the manager of Manchester United. One person who did leave was John Gidman, and you might think that I would have been relieved at that, but such was the unpredictability of the manager over the previous year I couldn't take anything for granted, particularly as Johnny Sivebaek was still there as a relatively fresh face.

We started the season as we'd ended it. Bryan Robson was missing with the shoulder injury he'd picked up in the 1986 World Cup and in his absence we fell to an opening-day defeat at Highbury. Worse was to follow as we lost two home games in a row again, this time to West Ham and Charlton. The rot had set in and time was running out – the club didn't trust Ron with money in the summer transfer window which was a huge sign in itself. They were calling upon him to prove himself to turn it around. Outwardly, Ron was not showing any signs of suffering under the pressure, but I had always been a bit wary of the bravado and wondered how real it actually was.

We drew at Leicester and then I was dropped – we won at home to Southampton but then lost against Watford, Everton and Chelsea in consecutive games. Six defeats in eight league games put us second-bottom.

I did feel sympathy for Ron but then this was a situation largely of his own making. Having tinkered with a winning team, he tried to spend to turn around a temporary run of bad form, and now was stuck with a bunch of players who either weren't good enough or had grown disillusioned with him. Perhaps he should have concentrated on sorting out that latter group, of which I was a part, but then maybe we'd all had enough and knew that there wasn't exactly a consistent disciplinarian route he would take. It was a situation out of control and one that ultimately he couldn't fix.

There had been a temporary upturn in form in October where we won three games in a row, and then drew three, but a 4-1 battering at Southampton in the League Cup put the writing well and truly on the wall.

The next morning at The Cliff, there was a pretty quick announcement. We were gathered in the gym and Ron came bouncing down the steps, trying to be as lively as he ever had been. There was a bit of nervousness as he announced he'd been let go, and then he went around the group shaking our hands.

In typical fashion, Ron threw a party that night and invited the players to go. I can't speak for who went or didn't, I just know that I didn't turn up. Why do it? It didn't make any sense. I wasn't particularly disappointed that he'd gone and wouldn't have attended one of Ron's parties anyway.

As for what it meant for me, well, for once, it meant that having to re-establish myself was an opportunity rather than a challenge. I'd broken into the team relatively late, then had to prove myself after Dave Sexton had been sacked, and then once more after John Gidman arrived. I had been deemed surplus to requirements by Ron with the acceptance of the Everton bid but I never wanted to leave United so it was something of a reprieve.

I always found the circumstances around the sacking of Dave and Ron fairly interesting. Dave had ended with a good run so why was he sacked without getting the chance to build on that? Conversely, Ron had ended with a really poor run yet had got a few more months at the start of the following season. Perhaps the board felt that the new signings might prove themselves with a little more time.

The squad that Ron had put together had been successful and as recently as a year previous had looked virtual guarantees to win the league. As FA Cup holders, we certainly had the quality to challenge, so it would be reasonable to assume that a new manager could come in and get us to those heights again with a bit of time. I was 27, approaching or at what should be my peak, and after so many near misses I was desperate to win the league with United. There were players like Robbo, Paul McGrath and Gordon Strachan at similar ages who were as good as anyone. I had no regrets over turning down Everton even though I could've won a league medal with them because it wouldn't have meant the same to me as winning it with United. They were my club, the only place I'd played and the only place I wanted to play.

Far from challenging for honours, in November 1986 people were saying, 'They're too good to go down.' Then again, they said that in 1974 and look what happened. We had no God-given right to be in the First Division and the turnaround in form since Christmas had been awful, there's just no other way of putting it. But for goal difference we would have gone from top of the league on New Year's Day to bottom of it in less than 11 months. It's an achievement but not the type we'd like to be associated with.

There was one obvious name who was mentioned in connection with succeeding Ron, the man who eventually got the job, but as players we were the same as anyone in being in limbo while it wasn't official. I'd learned from the episode with Dave being sacked not to really pay any attention to the press and thankfully we didn't have to wait too long until Alex Ferguson was installed as the new manager.

Ferguson came with a fantastic reputation for his achievements with Aberdeen in Scotland but the speed in which he was appointed may have come as a surprise to some. I'm sure it was something that had been given due consideration by the board and was probably on their minds since the summer and you would have to assume that conversations had taken place in advance for the move to happen as quickly as it did.

I've only seen Ron once since he was sacked – there was a legends game down at Evesham, and Ron was cutting the tape for their new ground. We said hello and that was that – I would certainly never ignore him or be unpleasant to him because as much as I disagreed with some of his decisions, he was just doing what he thought was right as a manager. That said, I was once asked who I would like least to be stranded on a desert island with, and I said Ron!

I did feel a little for him when he was later caught in controversy for alleged racist remarks – I certainly know from my experience with him that he isn't that way. It's not nice to see those kind of incidents but equally, when you're being paid for people to listen to you give your opinion, you are responsible for what you say and have to be aware of that. As a manager and a personality I wouldn't say he was one of my favourites – in fact, I cringed when he defeated United with Sheffield Wednesday in the 1991 League Cup Final, not so much because United lost but because of all the furore that would have been made about Ron afterwards – but I do have to give some credit where it's due, because the fact of the matter was that I played my best football under Ron and we had some great times as a club and team under him.

Nonetheless, Ron's sacking brought an overwhelming feeling of relief and rebirth, the proverbial fresh page for United to start again.

13

A Legacy Is Born

ALEX Ferguson arrived at Manchester United with a very impressive CV, which, you could say, gets even more impressive as time goes on. His Aberdeen side in the early 1980s were the first team to break the duopoly of the Scottish Premier Division by Celtic and Glasgow Rangers for 15 years, which was extraordinary enough, but he then went on to make them arguably the best team in the country over the next few years. And, since he left, it's been Celtic and Rangers ever since.

Ferguson also took his team to European glory by defeating Real Madrid in the European Cup Winners' Cup Final of 1983, which underlined his credentials as a great manager and the ideal candidate to replace Ron Atkinson. I personally hadn't had any meetings with him prior to him taking over at Old Trafford, with the closest I'd come probably being that missed opportunity to face Aberdeen with the way the draw went for the Cup Winners' Cup in 1985.

The way he spoke to the players and outlined what he thought was going to happen – and what he wanted to happen – made a very good first impression. With certain managers in recent years such as Louis van Gaal, Pep Guardiola, David Moyes, Jose

Mourinho and Sam Allardyce, a style of play instantly comes to mind for each of those managers whether you find that style aesthetically pleasing or not. It's a philosophy of football they've taken to different clubs throughout their career, they have conviction in their opinion of the way that football should be played and believe it will bring success.

When Alex Ferguson arrived we weren't entirely sure what his philosophy was with regards the current players. And although he spoke well, and seemed like a really mild-mannered individual, there were always a few comments of, 'Well, you've not seen the real Ferguson yet, the other side of him.' That made me curious rather than wary – after all, he had the pedigree behind him to back up his behaviour. I suppose that even as a manager, the man in control, he wanted to create a good impression and be friends with most while he established himself. I suppose that might surprise some who know Sir Alex, as he became, as someone who went by his own rules, trusted his own judgement, and couldn't care less what others thought of him.

I'm not going to contradict that as such, as there can be no doubt he was putting into place what he wanted to, but the first impression was created by the attention he gave us. He would talk to us in a group and then speak to the players individually about his thoughts of how we should be training and living – it was the first time I'd experienced that. That was his manner and his way of doing things, and it came across as him trying to make a good impression, but looking back you can see that these are the things that many people have said about him even in the last year of him being in management and probably right up to the last day.

The way he engaged you made you feel included and as if everybody would be getting their chance to prove themselves, and that provided a much-needed boost in morale.

There was one group meeting I recall down at The Cliff where he made a point about speaking about the way we lived and I think that was probably to do with the so-called 'drinking group' at the club and putting down a message right from the off. I have to say once more though that in comparison with what we knew went on at other clubs I didn't think we were any worse and as professionals I am certain that we all knew what we should and shouldn't be doing but, to return to another earlier point, we can only logically assume that without the drinking culture we'd inevitably have been better. And this speech delivered by our new manager was an early indication that he was going to seek to eliminate the culture, or at least reduce it. He wasn't wielding a big stick, but being up front about what he wanted, which was most certainly a positive thing.

When you look at the situation for what it was, and consider that all the change under the last year of Ron's reign was very much a bad thing, it's funny how the arrival of a new manager can make change seem like a good thing.

I suppose my first impression of the new man was so good because I found his personality a refreshing change – he wasn't so much quiet as methodical, and his intent was very much on improving the team rather than being one of the lads.

I've often thought about what he must have been planning in those early days because while it became evident he was outlining a long-term strategy which involved fundamental changes from top to bottom, in his mind, I'm sure he must have thought that it needed to be done quickly.

He must have been under quite a substantial amount of pressure early on. After all, he inherited a squad where a lot of players were either just at or just past their peak, and it was a large squad too. He had some big decisions to make with regards who to keep and who to move on – I'm sure the board would have wanted to see either a financial return or success on the pitch in return for the amount of money that Ron had spent.

Two days after taking over at the club, Ferguson took charge of his first Manchester United match as we travelled to Oxford United. I was given an instant boost by being selected for his first game in my usual position of right-back. I don't know how much he'd seen of the club beforehand or how much he knew of me but the side he put out against Oxford was a good, solid, established line-up with the likes of Moran, McGrath, Arthur, Frank and Remi. Norman and Bryan were injured which was of course a blow but just as big a problem was the fact that the established players had not got the opportunity to play as the cohesive unit we'd proven ourselves to be just 12 months before.

We lost 2-0 which was a very disappointing start but probably showed more of the existing problems which the manager had inherited. Often when a new manager comes in, his team respond accordingly and lift their game, but that wasn't the case – the manager thought that we looked tired, that perhaps we hadn't been training hard enough, or perhaps there were tired legs from the World Cup.

I didn't have that problem and I was still as fit as I'd ever been. I felt I lived right so I was hoping that it was noted by the manager and that I'd impressed him in that respect, despite the defeat. I certainly felt somewhat invigorated by the opportunity and the fresh atmosphere around the place and going by the fact that it took a while for him to make any notable changes to the playing personnel, I think that Alex was aware he had inherited a squad capable of challenging for honours, that we were just one or two players – and confidence – short rather than in requirement of wholesale changes.

In training, Ferguson didn't necessarily re-invent the wheel, but there was more focus on the players and form rather than the atmosphere. While Ron didn't neglect the responsibility of managing Manchester United, Alex, arriving fresh, reinforced the message of what that meant. We'd walk past the photographs of Best, Law and Charlton on the walls of The Cliff and he would be saying to us that we should be the next team to have our faces on the wall. He would say that we shouldn't use it as ghosts to haunt us, rather, figures to inspire us. 'The next group of players to win the First Division will be known as legends at this club,' he once said. I remember the words as clearly as anything. It was music to my ears and all the incentive any of us needed, if we needed any to begin with. It was a great motivational tool.

Would Ferguson have given the players as much time as he did if Ron hadn't spent so much money? Maybe not, but it's worth remembering that we were a good side when our strongest XI was out there. I'm sure it was a challenge that the manager relished.

The Oxford game, as unremarkable as it was at the time (the defeat was one to instantly forget), is remembered to this day as the first game of an incredible era of management. The teamsheet of that game, handwritten by the manager, sold for £19,500 at a 2013 auction. That was more than we earned in two months. Well, more than I did – I wasn't about to question anyone else's wages and I don't think I was ever the kind of player who would shatter the wage ceiling at the club! And I was a local lad. I can remember other players who had come through the system always moaning how little we were paid in comparison to the players who were brought in. When Norman left for Everton I think he said he had trebled his pay. Don't get me wrong, it was good money, and compared to the average wage in the UK we had it good, but in comparison in football it was pretty poor. Contract negotiations were always fairly straightforward, I never had a representative or agent so I would just go and see the manager when I felt I had deserved a new deal. Steve Coppell had always been good for giving advice on those matters.

I wonder how that teamsheet got out. Tommy Cavanagh used to come in with the opponents' sheet before a game and say, 'This lot are shite!' before throwing it to the ground. So who got hold of this one? Did the referee keep it? Strange that someone kept that particular sheet from what is essentially a fairly nondescript game.

Things didn't start great for Ferguson on the pitch although they were an improvement from how it had been at the start of the season. With such a big squad, he had a responsibility to give those players the opportunity to prove themselves, and that included the names that Ron had brought in that weren't quite of the standard that was required to improve us. Fortunately for me, I managed to keep my place in the team more often than not while these different teams were being fielded. I was at left-back in the game when the manager got his first win and it was Sivebaek who scored the first goal of Ferguson's United reign, against QPR.

Towards the end of December, Ryan, our second child, came along. Christmas is always a busy time anyway whether you're in football or not. When Karen went into hospital, Ashley needed looking after so the in-laws stepped in for us while I would go to work in the morning and then take him to visit Karen in the afternoon. This proved to be the case over the Christmas period as I picked Ashley up on Christmas Eve, wanting him to wake up on Christmas Day in his own house. After all the presents were opened it was off to work with the ground staff at The Cliff keeping an eye on Ashley while we trained. It was then straight to the hospital for a flying visit. Karen had prepared a lot of meals, including our Christmas dinner, but when I asked Ashley what he wanted, he replied, 'A cheeseburger!' So it was cheeseburgers for Christmas dinner. Maybe that's now why he loves having Christmas dinner at any time in the year. I ought to add – we did have Karen's dinner later on! After that, I had to take Ashley back to the in-laws and meet up with the team at the hotel.

United had a fairly decent Christmas period. I was rested for a game against Leicester but was in midfield for our Boxing Day trip to Anfield. I'm not blowing my own trumpet here, well, maybe I am, but I put in a great performance and really felt I contributed to a fine 1-0 win that we earned thanks to a Norman Whiteside goal. After the game we came out for a warm-down on the pitch which we didn't always do. A few of our supporters had been kept in and probably thought we'd come back out to say thanks for their great support. As fantastic as it normally was, we were due to play Norwich City the day after, so were just preparing for that.

We had played Liverpool off the park and then lost 1-0 to Norwich and I guess that really did sum us up. The problems that existed in our very best times under Ron were still there and were once again highlighted by Norwich City of all teams.

Before facing Manchester City in the FA Cup in January the manager took us away to Grasmere in the Lakes for a few days to get away from the chaos of the build-up in the city. It worked to an extent as we got the result – courtesy of another Whiteside goal – but we didn't particularly play well. We went out in the next round to Coventry City which was totally disappointing.

It was new territory for us to be out of every competition and so low in the league at the end of January. The manager deserved some credit for stabilising our form and taking us up to 13th but we were disappointed in ourselves for what was still under-performance to us. Low on confidence, Anfield aside, we didn't play particularly well most of the time.

I did have some conflicting emotions about my own place in the side. I was pleased to be playing although to be selected often at left-back was strange. I was out of my comfort zone but I also felt so embarrassed to be taking over from Arthur Albiston as he had been a magnificent player for the club and to my mind he still had plenty to offer, too. Nonetheless, I had to adapt and must have been doing well enough to keep my place in whatever position the manager trusted me to play in.

One thing that hadn't changed was that wherever we went and whoever we played against, we were still their biggest game of the season. Going back to that earlier time when we watched Liverpool play at Luton, the flipside of that for opposing teams is that when they get a full home crowd, it naturally spurs them on to raise their game, and maybe with us not quite being at our best, there was a sense of expectancy that they could take advantage and claim a famous result of their own. If even Liverpool behaved that way to play against us, then we had to expect it from anyone. Whatever the reason, we didn't win another away game after winning at Anfield in the 1986/87 season. Typical of us, though, we defeated Liverpool in the return with Peter Davenport scoring a late winner, and defeated City in the league derby at Old Trafford too.

Our year ended with four games in a week – we lost at home to Wimbledon and got battered 4-0 at Spurs, before drawing at Coventry City and welcoming Aston Villa to Old Trafford for the last match. It had been a hit-and-miss start to life under the new manager but there were a few players who were coming out of the season with credit. Dav had scored a fair few goals while Bryan, when fit, had been his usual self, and Gordon Strachan got a fair few too. I felt as if I had emerged from this difficult time with credit as well as I'd been influential in our forward play in the last few weeks of the season, setting up Strachan's goal at QPR and then playing a pivotal role in our

3-1 win over Villa. I scored our second when I was put through – my first effort was saved, but I converted with my left foot on the rebound and performed my customary forward roll. A couple of minutes later, I set up Bryan with a quickly-taken free kick to seal the result.

The win took us up to a final place of 11th which, looking at how low we were in November, represented a fairly decent turnaround, but we had stuttered in mid-table since January. We didn't need to be told that we should have done better overall but it was mentioned, at the end of the season, that more was expected of us next year.

14

'The best way to kill time is to work it to death.'

Anon

I THOUGHT somebody was on a wind-up when I discovered United's first signing under Alex Ferguson was Viv Anderson. Another right-back, and an England international to boot. Viv signed from Arsenal and was joined by Brian McClair, the highly-rated Scottish striker who our manager had seen at close quarters.

However, all those things that I'd once considered a hindrance – a new manager coming in, and playing out of position – were now counting in my favour. My versatility and fitness must have been considered favourably by the boss as in the season to come I would play more games than I had for a few years.

Viv's arrival was countered by the departure of John Sivebaek – additionally, Frank Stapleton and Terry Gibson were allowed to leave, to Ajax and Wimbledon respectively. Frank was probably just at the right time for him, having served United well. What was certainly encouraging was the calibre of players now coming in.

Pre-season went quite well for us, with McClair and Anderson among the goals in our short tour of Denmark. Well, I say it went well, but I mean results-wise, because I was in the wars a bit. I played the first pre-season game but then broke my collarbone so I flew back early with Colin Gibson.

We then faced Manchester City in the Manchester International Football Tournament and I had recovered to take my place. City had been relegated the previous season and so in the absence of a competitive fixture, we looked forward to the match as competitive was something it certainly was going to be. I learned that the hard way – I was competing with Paul Stewart for the ball, fairly I might add, when all of a sudden this dirty great elbow comes and strikes me under the eye. I had to go off and get stitches, and then later had to go to get my teeth fixed as it had smashed my mouth too. Neil Midgley, a local referee, had apparently agreed beforehand not to send anyone off. Paul said later that he was a little frustrated by things at the club and he took it out on someone. It just happened to be me. Neil ordered City to take Paul off. Those stitches seemed to take forever.

I went to the dentist the morning after and played against the Brazilian team Atletico Mineiro later the same day. Of course the City game had been lively but it was nice to play against foreign opposition which we were obviously unable to do because of the ban. Normally you're wishing pre-season away and although I wouldn't quite say we loved it now, I think we just enjoyed the change.

Brian had been brought in to score goals and he certainly did that. It had been said that we had been lacking in that kind of potency since Mark Hughes left although the fact that Brian scored so many and we still, at times, struggled, showed that the problems were a little deeper. It was a move in the right direction, nobody could contest that. Viv brought a fantastic pedigree and also was a great character – I suppose an outsider would say that he was one reason I didn't get as many England caps. He was a fierce competitor and one we always noticed when we played against Arsenal. The one thing that his signing did mean for definite was that he was going to be the first choice right-back and my position would have to be elsewhere.

Before, under a different manager, I might have had cause to be apprehensive, but with Alex Ferguson, I always felt comfortable in the belief I would get chances. And so it proved. You're not untouchable and you understand the way that football evolves but at United you always want to see the manager wanting to bring in the best players. If the player coming in is direct competition for your place in the team then it's up to you to raise your game, that's the way it has to be at all clubs. If you've got anything about you you're not going to just sit back and let it happen. It was reassuring that there was a clear purpose and direction to the manager's transfer policy, even with the failed attempt to sign Watford's John Barnes, who went to Liverpool. It was a statement to say that United were able to compete with anyone in the transfer market.

In another world I might have ended up playing behind John as I was at left-back at the start of the season. That meant time was just about up for Arthur Albiston and I must admit that emotionally I did find that a little difficult. It was different to succeeding someone in the first team – such as Jimmy Nicholl, for example. Arthur was someone who had essentially taken the exact same journey I had through the club's system and played on the other side of the pitch to me for nearly a decade. We had enjoyed all of our professional successes together and endured the low points.

I had, and have, so much respect for Arthur. You could probably name the number of bad games he had for the club on one hand and this was someone who had played over 400 times. In a period of underachievement for the club, nobody could question that we had a top-class left-back who had given exemplary service at the highest level year in, year out. I still thought he was capable of doing so. In a way, it was embarrassing that I was being selected ahead of him. Ultimately you have to look after yourself and I was never going to say 'no' to being selected. On one occasion I did try and broach the subject with him and tell him how embarrassed I was by it all, but he was typically dignified in his response, telling me that it was just football.

Positionally, it did take a little getting used to. I'd played in a number of positions and left-back was probably the most awkward, primarily because I'm right-footed, although I felt more than capable of using my left. I don't think I was ever caught out and I'd like to think that going forward, as I still liked to do, I was able to bring another dimension to our attacking play. I was able to use the experience that I'd gained from playing at centre-half with Kevin Moran, as he played on the right side of central defence. If you're against an opponent you naturally want them over on your stronger side and that's probably the biggest difference with regards your balance. You have to adapt but something else that helped me was that whenever I went off the ground, I would always use my left foot for that elevation. It had always been the same, whether it was doing athletics when I was younger or now, jumping for headers. I suppose it's the same as anything, but it was a lot easier with the ball than without. I was kept there for a while so I must have done something right. It may well be that on a subconscious level I was concentrating more because it wasn't my natural position and so the errors that might have come from my natural game at right-back were not there because of the extra caution I took.

It wasn't a bad team that Ferguson had inherited and with the boost of the new players coming in, we started the season really well, drawing two and then winning the following three of our opening five fixtures to go top of the league at the end of August.

One of those wins was at Charlton where I picked up another battle wound – perhaps with that positional adjustment coming into play, I'd stooped a little low for a header, and had taken a kick in the head. I've got a picture of me in this game, with a head full of Vaseline. Archie Knox said to me at half-time, 'You should have just kicked it away.' These things happen in threes so they say, and that was most definitely the case for me, with the previous injuries so far that season.

Expectations at United are high, and that is always the case, regardless of how disappointing recent times had been. You want to win the league every year but it was probably unrealistic to suggest that we would be challenging so soon after the period we had had. There was a lot of pride hurt by our mid-table finish but the table never lies, and we had to prove ourselves once more. I knew I was personally heading into a period of my career when it was now or never.

Though I was part of it, I don't think Alex had settled on his first-choice 11 and maybe that was the cause for some inconsistency which saw us drop to fifth and sixth place. We were picking up a lot of draws but if you were to take the positive from that, we were now a lot harder to beat.

My 300th game for the club came that November, in a draw at Upton Park. It was something I didn't really acknowledge at the time because even with 300 appearances for Manchester United under your belt, you can't rest on your laurels. You have to push on and improve or maintain your performance. You're as good as your last game, that's all there is to it. I would like to think that is the kind of attitude that the manager wanted from his players anyway. That's the way you have to think when you're a player.

Looking back, it's something I'm immensely proud of. When you go through the process of putting a record like your autobiography together you go over these kind of accomplishments and I suppose that is the right time to appreciate them in the context they are in historically. When you're coming into the game as a 15- or 16-year-old, just to be at Manchester United is incredible and then just to get into the first team is something you can't believe. If someone had said I'd spend 14 years at the club I'd never have believed them, a snotty-nosed kid from Accrington would play for this club that is a legend of the game.

In the process of writing my book, Patrice Evra surpassed my appearance total, moving on to 379 before moving to Juventus. That put me into 36th place in the list of most appearances which may seem low but when put into the context of Ryan Giggs with 963 and Sir Bobby Charlton on 758, it's just an absolute honour that I don't think I could justifiably articulate. I feel very lucky to be included among these kind of names and to be someone who came through the club, too.

Around half of the players to have played more times than me have come through the club's youth system and that gives an idea of the kind of integrity of that record and what it means.

The club is so illustrious that I see myself at 36th place, I look at the names that have been at the club and think you could probably name 40 – at least – who could justifiably be labelled a 'legend', if you're going by the criteria of football in general and not confining it to Manchester United. If you asked nine out of ten United supporters of a mixture of ages to name a list of 40 legends then I don't think I'd get a mention. Similarly, I don't think I'd get in anyone's best ever United XI. Without wanting to sound big-headed, if only for the number of times I played, I suppose I'd be mentioned in the debate for who would be selected at right-back, and even just to be mentioned in that regard is an incredible honour.

I'm not trying to pull myself down, I just don't think I'd be in that sort of company, but in a way that makes me feel prouder to be at that position in the list of appearances. Many players have played fewer times than me and will be declared as having done more. Eric Cantona and Cristiano Ronaldo are just two examples. There is a perception that personality and the position they played influences that opinion and I'm okay with that. I'd probably agree. One list I am top of is the one of appearances in the 1980s, which was another thing I've learned in recent years. That surprised me too when you think of Kevin Moran, Arthur Albiston and Bryan Robson.

It's difficult to single one reason out why the club have been so prolific at developing young players and giving them so many opportunities. Maybe it's easier to instil the desire and what it means to represent Manchester United into a developing young man rather than expect someone, an outsider, to come in and just understand straight away. It can overwhelm some who do come in as I knew. We'd continued to be successful in this with the players I've already mentioned, and Clayton Blackmore who had broken into the team and was doing really well. Where our issue was, was that these were staggered by maybe one a year, and that was something that the manager had been seeking to rectify behind the scenes. That paid off famously in 1992 with about half a dozen breaking through to the first team. I'd love to see something like that happen at United again. Now that group of players was a group of legends.

The flipside of being where I am in the list of appearances means that I'm one of those few to have played so many times and not won a league title. Sammy McIlroy and Arthur, Lou Macari, Martin Buchan are some who share that. I can sit here and pontificate over whether the timing was just off for me but then you have to look at both sides of it and say that with other things, the timing was right. I had problems with my appendix at a time when I wasn't sure if I would be kept on. If it hadn't been for that, would I have even been at United to have played as often as I did?

The way I look at it is that I am very privileged that there are a number of absolute legends and people who have accomplished so many great things. I've been able to play with, play under and sit and talk to some of these great people and those are experiences I treasure. It's funny because I'm writing this part of the book on a day when I've given a lesson at school about the difference between bragging, boasting, and being proud of something. It's only on reflection and being told all these different things and numbers that I take stock of what I did as a player.

In November 1987, 300 was just a number and it was something that was in the past as soon as it had happened. And though a league winner's medal was the top of my wish list, I wasn't expecting it to come this soon, particularly as Liverpool were seemingly running away with the title. They were scoring for fun and without European football, the First Division was all they had to concentrate on, and they were doing it with some style, scoring at a rate of almost three goals a game. It made for a strange division that year. First is first and second is nowhere, so the saying goes, but with no European places on offer, it made for a weird competitive environment.

That may go some way to explaining the FA Cup wins of the time. Coventry City had won it in 1987 and Wimbledon would famously go on to win it in 1988. The unpredictability of these games was probably at its peak because there were so few prizes on offer and the one off-games made for great occasions. With teams like ourselves, and Everton, once the league looked out of reach, I suppose it may have been difficult to instantly flick a switch and magically create the kind of intensity for a one-off cup game. That may well have been what caused Liverpool's defeat in the final of 1988 too.

Intensity wouldn't be an issue for us against Liverpool and we got a draw against them at Old Trafford. They were unbeaten coming into the game and took the lead but Norman equalised. One on one, the difference in quality in the teams and squads was not discernible to me and it might sound stupid, or maybe I just believed so much in the ability of my team-mates, I never thought they were really any better than us. I must be wrong on some level because while I had been a professional they'd won four league titles and they would go on to win another this year but man for man we'd always match them. Our star man on the day was not Norman but Gary Walsh, a local lad who'd broke through to play in goal. He made a couple of great saves to add to his really impressive start.

We lost to Wimbledon but at the end of November we flew out to Bermuda to play a couple of friendly games. The trip was remembered for the incident where Gary received a terrible bang on the head after a clash with a player which really set him back. That was in a game against Somerset Trojans where the assistant manager Archie Knox played and scored an absolute belter of a goal. The manager came on as well, right near the end. We must have been down to the bare bones! The atmosphere wasn't very pleasant and I don't think it was one of our most successful tours – certainly not for Clayton Blackmore, who ran into trouble when a local girl accused him of rape. Thankfully he was released without charge but it must have been horrible for him.

Happier times awaited us at home as we immediately agreed a deal to bring Steve Bruce to the club from Norwich City. This was a real boost as Steve was a quality defender and I couldn't wait to play alongside him. He broke his nose in one of his first games for us but that was the kind of player he was – he was always going to put his body on the line and into positions which may hurt. He was wholehearted on the pitch though I'm not sure I could say the same for him in training! I suppose he was saving himself for Saturdays, and his methods didn't turn out so bad, did they?

Our trophy pursuit was more or less over by February. We were defeated by Arsenal in the FA Cup and suffered a League Cup exit to Oxford. Defeat at Norwich – only our fifth of the season, mind you – on 5 March put us an incredible 17 points behind the still-unbeaten Liverpool. When it came to our return game with the leaders on 4 April, they had lost twice, and we'd closed the gap to 11 points, though they had two games in hand. They knew that with victory, a 14-point gap was essentially game over – we would only have 15 left to play for, while they would require only two points from 21 left available to win the league.

Even with that sense of inevitability come what may, there was no way we were going to lay down. There was no way we were going to be beaten though sadly it wasn't the best game for me personally. We scored early on through Bryan Robson but goals from Beardsley, Gillespie and McMahon in the space of eight minutes either side of the half-time break turned the game around. Clayton and myself were brought off for the attacking talents of Jesper Olsen and Norman Whiteside and it proved to be the right decision from the manager. At 3-1 down, Colin Gibson was sent off, but there was never any time we entertained the thought of defeat. Maybe that crept into the Liverpool psyche as we came back in style, with Robbo getting a second. Gordon Strachan equalised and then performed that famous 'cigar' celebration. He was a character in his own right and one who divides opinion. I found him personally to be okay and I thought he was a really good professional, though we never connected on a social level. He was an excellent player, though. It was a nice moment but ultimately counted for nothing.

Liverpool went on to win the league with one of their greatest teams. We could at least say that they couldn't beat us but given the choice of that or the champagne and league title, we'd all have swapped places with them in a heartbeat. At the end of the season that 17-point gap was down to nine which again was a huge leap from the previous season and even further from November 1985 but still some way from where we wanted to be. After the game at Anfield we won our remaining five league games which, again, considering the way we had been ending seasons, was a huge step in the right direction.

There was envy rather than jealousy regarding the achievements of our local rivals but that shouldn't detract from what we had done in a short space of time. Or rather, what the manager had done. We had at least proven to ourselves that we weren't as bad as it seemed we were when Ron was sacked and who knows what might have happened if Alex Ferguson had convinced John Barnes to join us instead.

On a personal level, I could hardly have been happier. I had played all but one of the games that season, albeit in a number of different positions. In fact, it's only through the accomplishment of what was admittedly a great Liverpool team that the 1987/88 season is included in the period of under-achievement. We had 81 points from 40 matches and only lost five times – in any other year, that would have been title-winning form, and I think that sometimes that is conveniently forgotten by those who think that the early years of Ferguson's reign were all dark days.

So what were we lacking? Not a goalscorer, for sure – Brian McClair had got 31 in 48 games. We'd made Old Trafford just about as much of a fortress as what Liverpool had made

Anfield. They ended with 15 wins and five draws at home while we had 14 wins, five draws and just one defeat. They had been remarkable on the road, although our record wasn't that bad.

We were positive and confident moving forward and the manager had already made astute signings which closed the gap. Our focus in the summer of 1988 was to prepare to take that extra step and finally become champions.

15

Chasing Shadows

BEFORE the pre-season break commenced we were given the opportunity to test ourselves against arguably the best side in Europe. AC Milan came to town with Marco van Basten and Ruud Gullit in tow. I spoke briefly about this match earlier – while a great test, it was an awful game, as we were played off the park. The pitch was in awful condition after the long season, really threadbare and unpredictable, but it made no odds to the Milan players who were flicking the ball up and volleying it around. It was almost literally jaw-dropping to observe their technical ability. Not only were we given a lesson in football but also in how to adapt to difficult circumstances.

Italian football had been renowned for its cynicism and gamesmanship but was now moving into that era where it was the eminent force in football. Serie A was the place to be – I think what AC Milan's win at Old Trafford showed was that even without the European ban, they would have had the edge over English teams. They certainly proved their worth to the world when they won the following two European Cup finals, featuring in four out of six finals over the following six years.

Their 4-0 win over Barcelona in 1994, which was essentially the last hurrah of that great Milan side, was some way to bring down the curtain. In the summer of 1988 van Basten scored the goal that he would most be remembered for, a stunning volley for his country against the USSR in the European Championships. I think Arnold laid it on for him if I remember correctly. Despite having a good season behind me, my own international ambitions were long gone and I never thought I would be considered for selection for England. There was no disappointment, as I'd long come to terms with that.

Unlike Barcelona in 1994, we at least restored some kind of credibility to our scoreline against Milan, going 3-0 down and pulling back late consolation goals from Jesper Olsen and Brian McClair. Our own humiliation was probably greater the previous week when we went down 2-0 to Manchester City in a testimonial for the outgoing Arthur Albiston. City had failed to get promotion at the first attempt and any chance to play them was welcomed though the result was disappointing. Despite a plethora of guests coming on we should still have won. Maybe the pitch condition had something to do with it but good players ought to deal with most things, as Milan showed. Old Trafford never had a great pitch, though it wasn't as bad as Derby's Baseball Ground. By Christmas, most surfaces were more or less the same anyway.

The manager built on the progress of the previous season by adding Jim Leighton and Mal Donaghy and bringing back Mark Hughes from Bayern Munich. I felt they were good signings. Mal was someone I'd always been impressed by and although he was coming towards the end of his career, like Viv, he had plenty left in the tank and his experience was something worth bringing in. I always thought it was a mistake letting Sparky go, so I was delighted to see him come back. Jim was probably the one I knew least of but Alex had worked with him in Scotland

and he'd had his successes up there. With the injury to Gary Walsh, we still needed a strong goalkeeper, and as Jim was someone the manager trusted, our own confidence was there as the boss had been right with just about all of his major calls so far.

That feeling that he had earned the right to be trusted had been established and it could be said that it was the good work which he had already done which was taken into consideration when the tougher days came calling. Having had a year and a half with the club, Alex Ferguson now felt more confident to make a number of changes. Graeme Hogg and Chris Turner were sold. Later in the season, Jesper Olsen was sold and effectively replaced by Ralph Milne. This was one the manager got wrong but, a little like Garry Birtles, Ralph didn't seem like a terrible signing at the time. Ralph had got great reviews for his performances for Dundee United but never really seemed to settle in Manchester. He was a nice lad but didn't seem to be living right and it wasn't so much of a surprise that his career at United didn't take off in the way it might have. Ralph was one of a few left-sided players who'd come in and for whatever reason, failed to adapt. Mickey Thomas, in hindsight, was positively successful compared to the likes of Ralph. For what it's worth I think Arthur Graham, by comparison, could never really go down as a disappointment or a 'flop' as he was brought in to do a job for a period of time and I felt he did it admirably. He may have been purchased as a stop-gap and as it transpired, that was what he ended up being, but I do feel that his contribution was far greater than realised or he's given credit for.

The left side was obviously something that the manager was seeking to address. Jesper had one or two fitness concerns and, maybe, the boss saw something in Ralph which had attracted him to John Barnes the previous year, a little bit of an explosion which could turn a game on its head. Unfortunately for everyone concerned it didn't quite turn out that way. Ralph's problems followed him in later life and maybe he struggled with the weight of expectation.

Another player who could turn a game was Paul Gascoigne. This was the time when United infamously thought they had captured the young Newcastle star. As players we heard the rumours and thought it was going to go through and were disappointed when it didn't. Did money turn his head? Those reasons have been speculated over for years. There was some understanding when Barnes had chosen Liverpool from a footballing perspective even though I, with my bias accepted, would always think that anyone in football would choose United. Everybody knows what Gazza was like as a player and it doesn't need me to say he would have enhanced our team and taken us on to another level. Can you just imagine what a midfield of Gascoigne and Robson would have been like for United, and what it could have been like for England with that increased chemistry?

You can never say for sure but that would have been the strongest midfield in the league. People always wonder what he would have been like under Ferguson's tutelage but for me that's the $6m question isn't it? It was a big disappointment, as I say, when we didn't get him in.

Another player who left was Kevin Moran, who went to Spain shortly after having his testimonial, against Manchester City. I didn't play in that game but I was in a United XI that travelled to Hartlepool on the eve of the new season. It was a fairly decent side we put out – Paul McGrath, Norman Whiteside, and Chris Turner in goal, shortly before he left. I've honestly got no idea of what happened that day but we lost 6-0. Six-nil! What an absolute embarrassment, but it was just one of those days where everything went wrong. Thankfully it wasn't in competitive action.

I've heard it said that this was the game where the 'hairdryer' legend was born but to my mind that was after a defeat at Wimbledon's Plough Lane shortly after the manager's arrival in November 1986. Everything was a mess. There were no lights in the changing rooms, salt instead of sugar in the tea, all these little things Wimbledon were associated with. After the game, Alex came in and blasted the entire team. I was at number three on the day and he was going round one to 11 so I got one of the early rants – the best thing to do was to just stay quiet while he was right in your face, screaming and shouting. He went around the team, slightly calmer as he went on but still intensely aggressive for whoever he was bellowing at. Peter Barnes was in the bath while this was going on and didn't dare come out! You could hear the water swishing about as Peter just remained in there and eventually that was enough to give us all – manager included – a laugh. That's not to say that we didn't get the hairdryer at Hartlepool, just a note to acknowledge that he was confident enough to get in our faces essentially from day one. It was only a friendly but it was as big a blow to the pride as the defeat against Bournemouth in the cup.

I was just thankful that in the short term at least it didn't seem to affect my first-team chances. More than the significant personnel shift, it was noticeable that there was a certain kind of character coming in, perhaps best exemplified by the Donaghy/Moran switches. Kevin was still a hell of a defender but was part of the 'drinking club' while Mal was a seasoned professional who never seemed to miss a game. That's not to say that Kevin had a problem with drink or that Mal was teetotal in comparison, simply, an observation that I feel it was around this time that the manager was looking for a certain kind of character in his team and – again, for whatever reason – felt it was time for Kevin to move on. Kevin and Jesper had had their injuries but on talent alone I think nine out of ten people would select them over Mal and Ralph, but the manager was starting to put together his vision. To my mind, the outgoing players weren't any trouble, but it must have been in the manager's mind to move on from Ron's boys.

This was also the last year for Norman Whiteside and Paul McGrath. Norman struggled with injuries all year – we had a squad that could cope with the absence of a Whiteside or a Robson for one-off games but when you are missing the amount of games that Norman was, then you have to make a serious adjustment. Norman should really have been the left-sided player we craved but it was injury more than lifestyle that did for him – and it was a double blow, in a sense, that we brought in Ralph and he was unable to reach that level too.

As we'd learned under Ron, wholesale changes to the team when there's no tangible improvement can only have a destabilising effect. Having finished second the previous season the expectation was for us to kick on and really challenge for the title and maybe with a Gascoigne in our ranks we would have done, but the transfers that had been made were very much transitional rather than improvements, and that reflected in our results. I was a regular in the side until a 2-2 draw at Derby in November, which left us in 11th place.

The transition was not helped by the fact that we started to suffer an injury crisis. I was one of those missing through injury and with a few out, and results not going well, the dark clouds began to return over the winter of the 1988/89 season. It was tough for the manager as he was unable to simply throw more money at the squad but football is unforgiving. It's a results sport and even though we had logical reasons for why, this season, we were under-performing, ultimately the manager takes the responsibility and so it was inevitable that he would start to face criticism from the press with us languishing in mid-table.

It's difficult when you're in a helpless position as I was over the Christmas period. There's never – usually – a good time to be injured but I was 29, a player used in a number of positions, and with the manager under pressure, it would have been easy to wonder if, in fact, I would survive another transition period at the club. I wasn't a player who would have been identified as a problem with my fitness but I'd gone through so many struggles that the next one might be the last. My only thought at the time was to return to fitness and help the team climb the table and who knows, maybe it was that kind of attitude that meant I'd been kept at the club as long as I had. Like I say, though, over Christmas 1988, I was helpless to do anything except get myself fit. Having undergone an operation on my hernia, it was a lot easier said than done.

It was more necessity than choice which provoked the first 'Fergie's Fledglings' selection in the FA Cup tie against QPR. It was no secret that the manager was making changes to the way the youth system was run, with particular interest paid to scouting, but I'm sure he would have preferred another scenario in which to throw so many in at one time.

Lee Martin and Lee Sharpe were both talented players and would maybe have been pushing the senior players hard anyway but would Russell Beardsmore, Tony Gill, David Wilson and Deiniol Graham have been considered in normal circumstances?

Maybe with the way that the FA Cup is considered today, but I don't think so at the time. That said, it is a huge credit to those lads that they all put in great performances and got through the tie against QPR after a replay.

And one thing you have to give the manager credit for is giving those kids the opportunity rather than a short-term loan signing like a Cunningham or a Crooks. It was better for the legacy of the club in my opinion. The cup run was good for morale as it positively affected our league form – we went up to third at one point, before tailing off and dropping back into mid-table after a defeat at Nottingham Forest and a draw at home to Arsenal. Around the same time, Forest came to Old Trafford and ended our cup run with a 1-0 win. Another season effectively over by March.

The cup defeat against Nottingham Forest was the last time Gordon Strachan played for the club. I think there was a bit of a personality clash between Gordon and the manager and a move had been on the cards for a while. It was a good move for Gordon of course as he went on to win the league with Leeds United but it wasn't seen as a good move for us at the time as he was such an established talent. Russell Beardsmore's emergence as a solid player on the right-hand side clearly hastened the decision to move Gordon on.

Despite there being no trophies to compete for, there was plenty at stake for the players at United during the run-in to the end of the season. For me, I had to try and re-establish myself in a team that was still not quite settled. I was back on the bench for a very disappointing home defeat to Derby and came on for the last 20 minutes.

Had things worked out differently, and we had defeated Forest in the prior round, then we would have been the team facing Liverpool at Hillsborough in the FA Cup semi-final instead of slumping to an instantly forgettable loss against the Rams. Instead of going home, we had a long weekend staying with the team and travelling to the south coast, and I was rooming with Brian McClair. We were receiving sporadic bits of news about the events at Hillsborough but nothing was clear until we saw it unfold in front of our eyes on *Match of the Day* that evening. It was an absolute tragedy and a disgrace that it took so long for the truth to be admitted about the events of that afternoon.

The loss to Derby was one of six in our last eight games which is dreadful by anybody's standards, almost relegation form. Even with nothing to play for, performances shouldn't just drift off like that. I was back in the team and at right-back too but that wasn't even the slightest consolation for the way we ended the season. We seemed a million miles away from being in the kind of position Liverpool and Arsenal found themselves in for the final match of the season, facing each other with a winner-takes-all scenario at Anfield.

I was cheering on Arsenal the whole way through in a pub in Oswaldtwistle. I was far from an Arsenal fan but our professional rivalry with Liverpool meant that there was that edge there too. For the Gunners to win it in the way they did was incredible.

There have been debates in recent years about which way is the best way to win it – Manchester City won the 2012 title with almost the last kick of the game and Blackburn Rovers won it in similar fashion despite actually losing their last game (both times with United losing out) – but for me, the Arsenal win is as good as it gets, because that's against your direct opponents for the championship. Pure drama. Good for them, but nothing more than an empty feeling inside for us. That should have been us, we should have at least been challenging, but we were nowhere near.

It was now the second time in three years we'd finished in mid-table and despite it being a competitive division (and our mitigating circumstances), you can only return to the fact that the table does not lie. I still thought that behind the scenes, things were moving in the right direction. I maintained a belief that the manager was doing things right, even if part of that was the blind faith I always held in the club coming good regardless. I think that was in part down to the intent and attitude of the manager. We were in for the top players even if we'd missed out on a couple, and young players were getting the opportunity to prove their worth.

That's not to say that we were immune to the criticism that came with our end-of-season form. You try and shut yourself off, or you try and disassociate yourself from it if you aren't playing so often. Maybe some who weren't playing saw it as a positive as they thought the manager may be moved on. Transition was very much the key word around Old Trafford but there were huge question marks over whether Alex Ferguson would be the man charged with handling it for much longer.

16

'History never looks like history when you are living through it.'

John W. Gardner

I STILL insist that at the time, I was as concentrated on the present and future as I ever had been, particularly with things as they were at Manchester United. Thirty had always been seen as something of a milestone for players, an age when the physical peak has gone and they begin to become phased out of the team. I was approaching that milestone and with the hernia problem behind me I had it all to prove that I was as physically capable as I ever was.

However, for perhaps the first time in my career, I did indulge in something of a retrospective look at my time at United as I prepared for my testimonial.

I could have had it sooner, but Arthur and Kevin got there before me. By the time I finally had mine granted, I was in my 13th season at the club. On a personal note it was something to look forward to among the disappointment of the run-in.

The process of getting a testimonial may have changed these days but back in the 1980s it was pretty strange. The club didn't offer, you had to go and ask, so that's what I did. I went to see the manager around the time I was returning to full fitness and asked if it would be possible to have a testimonial. He asked how long I had been there and was surprised when I told him – he said he'd speak to the board and it wasn't long before he told me that they had accepted the request.

It was strange new territory for us so I approached the gentleman who had assisted in the testimonial of the cricketer Jack Simmon, Murray Bernie. We have a tenuous connection to Jack in that my mother-in-law is his wife's aunt – or something like that, so we asked Jack for his contact details.

The next thing was to sort out the opposition and it was still frowned upon to invite a top European club due to the Heysel ban still being in place (although that didn't stop the Milan friendly!), so I had to think of a team that I had some sort of connection with. My full debut had been against Manchester City, I'd also scored against them and captained United against them. Aside from the testimonials, we hadn't played them for a while, and it was thought that it would be best for a good crowd.

Murray advised us to put a committee together which consisted of around ten or 12 people. Margaret Riley, who I mentioned right at the start of this book, agreed to be secretary, and her husband Tony was on the committee. I approached my old deputy head to be the chairman, who was also a priest – Father O'Neill – and he had reservations about the commercial side of it. I tried to rationalise it by explaining that a few people would benefit and it wouldn't just be me, and that eventually went some way to convincing him to take part. David Meek, Gordon Clayton and Wilf McGuinness were also on board.

Put bluntly, a lot of attention is paid to attempting to raise as much money as possible within the testimonial year. There were obvious things like a sportsman's dinner, race nights, which we did. We tried to get supporters and players involved. It was an enjoyable time despite the on-pitch events at the club.

I suppose if you were to look at my career I wouldn't stand out as an obvious choice to go and request an event that would revolve around me. But at the time, it meant a considerable deal and was a good moment of recognition. I felt proud of what I had done at the club and felt I had given them good service. Yes, the club had given me so much, but I certainly felt I was deserving of the custom that other players received for similar length of service. As it was something that happened in football, I was comfortable with it.

Shortly after the announcement of the testimonial was made, Manchester City secured promotion back to the First Division, which didn't hurt our own promotion of the event too much as it was seen as a great build-up to the new season. It was our final pre-season game, after another Far East trip.

We were defeated 2-0 in the testimonial but the result was essentially meaningless – it was so nice to have my family become the centre of attention and to take the boys on a lap of honour around the pitch. They didn't realise what was happening and Karen was trying to get them to come down to the pitch before the end of the game in order to get them prepared. They didn't want to miss a kick! They were so young at the time, I think six and three, but they can still just about remember it, Ashley more than Ryan.

The crowd wasn't the biggest, around 20,000, but many who did come stayed until the end and we were very appreciative of that. We had a bit of a get-together afterwards where we gave the players a small token of our appreciation.

Despite my best intentions, all the furore around such an event meant that I naturally began to consider how long I had left. The concentration was there as well as the belief that I had plenty left to offer and I did of course at least have the confidence that when fit, the manager was normally including me in the team. However, the transition we were in had now left me with contrasting emotions. As good as it had been to be playing, the fact I didn't have a settled position left me wondering whether I was essentially there to plug the gaps in the team until someone better, or more suited to the role, came along. Was I really a first choice or was I making up the numbers? Nothing was imminent with regards a transfer so I was fairly confident that I'd be staying around although another busy summer on the transfer front meant that once more, nothing could be taken for granted.

Paul McGrath and Norman Whiteside were the big casualties. Paul went on to have success with Aston Villa but Norman's move to Everton was followed by an injury that forced him to retire.

Mike Phelan and Neil Webb had come in to boost our midfield (though Mike, like myself, could play a number of positions) and soon after the season started, Gary Pallister was signed from Middlesbrough to replace McGrath. The manager also finally got the all-action midfielder he wanted with Paul Ince from West Ham in September, after a protracted saga. Ince was followed by Danny Wallace a few days later. In all, the club had spent just over £8m on new recruits, showing a serious statement of intent.

Money was talking around Manchester United and was very much the theme on the opening day of the season. Businessman Michael Knighton had been rumoured to have agreed a takeover of the club from the Edwards family and as players it was a bit of a surreal time. We'd obviously already spent and were continuing to do so and were unsure what was actually happening behind the scenes. It seemed a little bit of an unnecessary circus which was not befitting of what I expected from Manchester United. We – or at least I – knew nothing about our potential new owner. I was just there to play football.

Knighton generated lots of publicity on the first day of the season as we were preparing to play Arsenal, taking to the pitch to perform some tricks with a football. What a load of bizarre nonsense. Did he see himself as a saviour of the club? It was a sideshow I'm sure the manager was not happy with, taking attention away from footballing matters to put the spotlight on one individual who wasn't even formally in charge.

We were oblivious as players, inside the changing rooms away from it all. It provided little distraction for us on the day as we battered Arsenal 4-1 and I was in the team at right-back. Steve Bruce got us off to the perfect start and Neil Webb got off to a flyer with a great goal on his debut. Everything seemed to go right for the team and personally, it was one of my best games for a long while. Afterwards, Lou Macari approached me having watched the game to compliment me on my performance. Arsenal came into the game as champions and our display showed just how good we could be on our day. We weren't just capable of beating teams, we were capable of battering anyone, which made the fact that we hadn't won a league title all the more bemusing. Perhaps our biggest opponents were ourselves, we were our own worst enemies.

Having survived the majority of changes under the manager, I was once again a regular, but that bright start was a false one as we lost three games in a row against Derby, Norwich and Everton. We crushed Millwall 5-1 which should have seen us with our tails up but then came the game which everyone still remembers, the Manchester derby at Maine Road. For the first ten minutes we were all over them. Some trouble kicked off behind one of the goals and the referee ordered us back into the changing rooms. We came back out shortly after and suffered the most bewildering experience. I swear they only had around five attacks but scored from each of them, by hook or by crook. It was a bad day for us all but particularly Gary Pallister who was in the spotlight, and Paul Ince. Reading 'City 5 United 1' on the back pages on Sunday morning was horrifying. Sometimes if you get a beating it's easier to take if you play poorly but I still insist that we didn't. We weren't worse than them on the day. We've probably beaten them playing poorer than that. At least Sparky scored the best goal of the game with a overhead kick. Small mercies!

It was, nonetheless, an iconic result which sent shockwaves and I think for the first time, suggestions that the manager would get sacked began to be taken seriously. That was the external view anyway – he'd spent a lot of money and that result, followed by a goalless draw at home to Sheffield Wednesday, saw us in 17th position. People were drawing comparisons with Ron but for me, the difference was that you could tell the players he had brought in were quality and just needed time. My preference was that Alex Ferguson should stay but there's no denying that it was touch and go for a while. The noises ever since from the directors are that his job was never at risk but the thought must have crossed their minds as we went into the winter period and lost four games in five in December.

Supporters had grown restless, something that was always going to happen when speculation was swirling in the press and things weren't going well on the pitch. Some people think that it's counter-productive to boo or protest but my view is that they have paid their money and they're entitled to express their opinion. It's human nature. Of course you'd like everyone to be positive and for the fans to get behind us as one in times of trouble but it's the way it goes. That said, as much as I feel people are entitled to do as they please, I'm not a particular fan of booing. I can't say that it ever negatively affected my performance but let's just say it didn't help. That was a shame when remembering the positive difference that supporters can make, such as when we played Barcelona in 1984. Large elements of it are understandable. You can't manipulate the circumstances that led to such a great atmosphere against Barcelona and, with that appreciation of how these things manifest themselves, it was easy to understand why so many were dissatisfied.

Things needed to change and ultimately I became a victim of that. The manager said at one point that he felt I'd 'lost my legs' after coming back from the hernia but I think what he meant was that I'd lost a little bit of pace. It is strange how these things work, I had made my debut in August of 1980 and was, more or less, first choice for the rest of the decade. As soon as the 1990s were here, I was out again! Time catches up with everyone but I was still disappointed to miss out on selection. Every Friday when that teamsheet went up and I wasn't on it the disappointment was as strong as it had been at any time prior. Perhaps, it may have even been stronger, as the realisation began to dawn on the long-term significance. At the time I wasn't looking at records but looking back, to have finished with 299 league games is a bit of a nuisance. But then, with 378 appearances overall, I guess I could say the same about that not quite being 400. It would have been nice to have double that amount.

From December onwards I wasn't first choice for league selection but found myself in contention for cup games. There is a slight tendency for people to revise the past when they look at the Nottingham Forest match in the FA Cup as the 'turning point' in the manager's reign. Mark Robins scored the goal that saw us qualify but it was not the best performance and in the next round against Hereford we laboured again. The pressure hadn't eased up any, the manager was still being threatened (at least in the press) with the sack, but nobody ever remembers that Clayton Blackmore scored with just minutes remaining at Hereford to see us through 1-0.

I would say that around the time of the Hereford tie, the pressure was at its peak. The Forest game had been followed by defeats to Derby and Norwich in the league, putting us back down in 17th place and leaving us without a win in the First Division for over two months. Looking at it from a general footballing point of view, defeat against Hereford would probably have seen Ferguson sacked, or at least it would have been the perfect excuse. Ultimately it's Mark and not Clayton who gets the credit for saving the manager.

The league was well and truly gone but although there was only the FA Cup to play for it wasn't as if the pressure was any greater to succeed in the tournament. Well, what I mean by that is that it wasn't noticeably any greater than what it normally was playing for Manchester United. Every game was that cliché of a cup final anyway. I had played every round in the cup, which included wins over the Uniteds of Newcastle and Sheffield, and after the latter, I found myself back in the team for league games against Everton and Liverpool. It was sod's law, then, that I picked up an injury that ruled me out of the semi-final against Oldham Athletic. I couldn't get back fit in time and was gutted to miss out. Absolutely gutted. I felt that if I was fit I would have been selected – and to compound that pain, not only did I miss the occasion of an FA Cup semi-final, but I missed taking part in a great spectacle that went to a replay. I wasn't even anywhere near taking part in the second game either. Mark Robins decided the tie with an extra-time winner that sent us to Wembley to face Crystal Palace and it was then all on for me to try and make sure I was fit for that.

I did all I could and after a couple of games in the reserves I made what turned out to be my final league appearance for the club at Nottingham Forest in our penultimate game. We lost

4-0 which was, of course, hugely disappointing, but the threat of relegation had disappeared with a run of four straight wins a few weeks previously.

I was, at least, in the travelling party that went to Wembley for the final. I roomed with Mal Donaghy who, like me, was contending for a spot on the bench with Clayton Blackmore. There was speculation on *Football Focus* at lunchtime about who would get the spot and it felt strange watching that with Mal in our room. We were team-mates in opposition. They named the likely teams and substitutes. They mentioned Mark Robins (whose goal threat meant he was always likely to be there) and then they said, 'The second substitute is likely to be Mick Duxbury.' Mal turned to me and said, 'You've got it Dux, well done.'

Perhaps for the best, I decided to not count my chickens just yet. We travelled to Wembley where the manager informed Clayton he would in fact be the substitute. I showed – or at least attempted to show! – the same kind of dignity that Mal had when I was congratulating Clayton. Inside, I was devastated. In my heart of hearts, knowing the way things had gone, I knew that was going to be my last game for Manchester United. To end in an FA Cup Final, even as a substitute, would have been a nice (and maybe some would say fitting if they were being kind) finish. It wasn't to be.

The final was another spectacular game, finishing 3-3 and going to a replay. I didn't get my hopes up for selection as I thought the manager would choose the same team but he did make one shock decision, dropping Jim Leighton and selecting Les Sealey in goal. Conceding three goals meant that if there was a change to make, it probably would come in defence, but it was still a huge shock and a bold choice regardless. Paul Ince was at right-back, unfamiliar territory for him, and if we were to put in a contrived argument, I might have been considered for selection there. There was no room for sentiment. Goalkeeper aside, the team remained the same, and the manager could say his decision was justified as Lee Martin scored and we won the cup.

I'm putting my selfish head on again here in admitting that I didn't share the satisfaction of my team-mates afterwards. I didn't feel part of the FA Cup-winning team. I know it sounds bad, and I didn't want United to lose. It's purely selfish. I didn't want anyone to have a bad game or get injured but I didn't feel anything. It was hard to take, admittedly selfish, and undeniably a gut reaction to being left out.

With it being a midweek game, we travelled back to Manchester afterwards, and the day after (or it may have actually been the day after that) Alex and I arranged to have a meeting about ten minutes away from where I lived. After the cup win, one of the directors had given him a watch, and he left his old watch on one of the changing room pegs. I said to Viv Anderson that I was going to nick it but I was only joking. I did take it as the manager had forgotten it and gave it back to him at the meeting. So much for gratitude, as he went on to tell me I was being released! There was no animosity. He was trying to give me advice and saying that he felt I was the kind of player who would need a big club. I was disappointed although I was at least self-aware enough to recognise it was coming and at least it had been dealt with face to face and honestly.

With that, my association with the club I'd been with since a schoolboy was officially over. Fourteen years. I've talked about numbers and it would have been nice to hit those higher landmarks and when you take into account the number of youth team, friendly and reserve games I played, I suppose I must have represented Manchester United in some shape or form well over 600 times. Would I have wanted more? In a perfect world, it would never end. I would have snatched your hand off for the time I ended up actually spending at what I feel is the biggest and best club in the world without question. I felt privileged but by the same token I also felt that I had justified my inclusion for as long as I had. I'm not interested in labels or comparisons even though compliments are nice. What means more to me is the experience I had, the fact of what I lived through and the club I played for rather than an objective or subjective opinion of how good I was.

All that said, it did feel like the right time to leave. The problem wasn't leaving. It was playing for another club.

17

Pastures New

I WAS very appreciative of the manager saying that he felt I could play for a top club but I had to be realistic. The first thing was that wherever I went from Manchester United was going to be a step down no matter where I went. The second was that, with a young family, I had a preference to stay in the north-west which automatically ruled out countless clubs. I had prepared myself for the probability that I might have to drop down a league but was hopeful that I wouldn't have to play any lower than the Second Division. Regardless of what I wanted, it was out of my hands to a major extent as it depended on who, if anyone, actually wanted to sign me!

Agents weren't as prominent in the game – a couple of the lads had them, but I hadn't, and I'd never used any in my contract negotiations. The PFA had their released list which went around clubs and that's how word was spread. United had been good with me and said that in recognition of the service I'd given, I'd be given a free transfer so wouldn't cost any suitors a fee. My contract was up anyway, to be fair, and the summer of 1990 was spent waiting for, but not getting, that phonecall.

The club still held my registration – I talked to the manager who said I could stay at the club if I wished, but was up front with me and said I wouldn't be playing the sort of games I'd been used to. I hadn't done any coaching badges and hadn't given any thought to that so I don't know if that was on his mind. I reported back to the club for training in pre-season which they let me do to keep my fitness up. Having come to terms with leaving after all that time, it was a little strange to be back around the club, but it did feel as if everything and everyone – including myself – had moved on.

Around the time of my testimonial a year earlier, Mel Machin, who had been in charge of Manchester City, had made a very informal enquiry about the possibility of me moving across town. I wasn't interested then but he moved to Barnsley and made another move once he realised I was without a club. I wasn't particularly keen as it was a little out of the area; Wolves showed an interest so I went and spoke to them. I was close to signing and more or less agreed terms but changed my mind late in the day with the locality once again the major factor. The last club to come in was Blackburn and I met Don Mackay, the manager. He wanted me to play left-back. I didn't exactly agree with that but mentioned it was funny as that was where I'd been playing under Alex Ferguson. Don offered me a contract and with everything more or less perfect with not having to move and the status of the club, I agreed to join.

Blackburn Rovers were in the Second Division but had narrowly missed out on a couple of promotion attempts in recent years, so I was satisfied that they were a club on the 'up'. I joined with positivity and what I would like to believe was the right attitude but the difference in going to play for Blackburn Rovers and Manchester United was profound. It wasn't just the size of the clubs, though that played a part, I think it was more the change itself. I'd gone from the only place I knew in the profession (and a place that I wasn't alone in feeling was the best) to somewhere new that wasn't quite the same.

Kevin Moran was there, as was Frank Stapleton, so there were familiar faces, but becoming detached from United had, in a way, detached me from football.

I still enjoyed the game, don't get me wrong, but it was like it had suddenly become a job. I was doing it for a living, rather than living to do it. Perhaps my character and personality didn't help as it had taken me a long time to really feel 'at home' at United, if that makes sense. It was taking a lot of getting used to and ironically I think that staying in the area compounded that problem. I was so used to my routine and that routine was dictated by Manchester United. Now, everything in my life was the same, except I was playing for Blackburn Rovers. That's not meant as a slight at my new club, I just mean that in retrospect, perhaps it would have been better for me to have taken the plunge and moved away.

Socially not much changed – Blackburn was closer so I spent more time at home. It also gave me the opportunity to indulge in a sport I'd really grown to love. I'd always been interested in British field sports and the great outdoors and since I was a young boy I'd spent plenty of time coarse fishing. However it was only when I got to the age of 30 that funnily enough, through Karen's brother Stephen, I first went fly-fishing. Over the years I have been able to spend more time doing it and can hopefully do so in the future. I just love being outside, and admittedly sometimes the solitude and escapism it offers from everyday life, as well as fishing itself. The times I do catch are a bonus.

I'd joined Blackburn on the eve of the season and was able to participate on a pre-season trip to Dublin a week before the kick-off. It was a lot to take in in a short space of time. In the week before kick-off, I had to attend a funeral. On the day, I switched my training around so that I could train with the youth players rather than the first team, and got injured, meaning I was out for the first few weeks of the season. My first game for

Rovers was ironically enough against Barnsley at Ewood Park in September, and sure enough, I was at left-back. I was, in a way, just satisfied to be playing, but the 2-1 defeat was still a blow to my professional pride. It was quite the culture shock.

It's natural that going from playing alongside players like Steve Bruce and Bryan Robson to, with all due respect, players in the Second Division, that it is difficult to adapt. You hope that you can influence others to raise their game but that's not easy. I was another year older, not as fit as I had been, and the team was struggling with a lot of injuries. Rather than promotion, we were engaged in a relegation battle, enduring mostly miserable runs in my early weeks and months at the club.

Blackburn didn't have their own training ground at that time so for training the players would pick each other up and go down to different local parks or even school playing fields. It was something to adapt to, that's for sure.

The one real bright spark of that season came in January when we were drawn against Liverpool, at home, in the FA Cup. We gave it a real good go and Simon Garner scored for us in the first half. They scored right at the death to equalise – it was one of the first goals of this nature to be scrutinised in such a fashion, as the ball boy threw the ball back to a Liverpool player quickly at a throw-in and we were caught out. It wasn't the ball boy's fault, I bet he felt terrible. Still, that was our big moment, as close as we were going to get. In the return at Anfield we were given a going-over by about three goals. If anything was going to remind me that I was no longer at United, it was losing at Anfield, which was something that I never did! It took back-to-back wins against Barnsley and West Ham in April to ensure safety in the division.

It was a world away from what was happening at United, with their glorious European Cup Winners' Cup campaign. Now away from it all, I was happy to watch them win and especially pleased for Sparky to score the winner. For myself, it was better that I was away trying to get first-team football rather than just hanging around hoping for the odd game, but it was hard to watch as it was almost in my face. Could I have made an appearance in that European campaign? Possibly. But I couldn't – and didn't – have any regrets over the move that I had made because I was a professional. It would have been letting myself down had I stayed, in a sense.

I didn't get any personal satisfaction from the club winning the FA Cup in 1990 so it wouldn't have felt like an accomplishment had I been around the squad for any other successes, whatever they may have been. Maybe it's different in the league because you play a certain number of games to qualify for a medal so you can value your contribution on that merit but I feel it would have been compromising my personal pride and values, those which had been so important to the success I had enjoyed, to contradict them now. I had come to terms with fighting for a place on the bench in 1990 but even that wasn't really me, or doing myself justice. All I have to do is remember how different I felt in winning the FA Cup in 1983 and 1985. Even in 1985 I felt less involved and I played that day, albeit as a substitute. I've nothing against players who do stay on with marginal involvement as it's their call and their life but it wasn't for me.

The only decision that I had any cause to consider was whether moving to Blackburn had been the right one but that's easy to say with hindsight. It was hard to see what we were going to do to progress – Don Mackay was a decent enough manager but there didn't seem to be much organisation or direction to the training, as in the week we seemed to just play games. There was a difference in intensity. It didn't translate well on the pitch, though the injuries we had in the squad played a part in our lack of consistency.

When I initially joined the club I was of the belief that they had the intention to get promoted; no club has a directive to get relegated or struggle but you can quickly ascertain the strength of ambition. The problems that were out of the manager's hands meant I wasn't going to question the ambition but it was clear that moving into my second year at Blackburn, the objective was for a vast improvement all round no matter what.

Not that it made any difference once August came around. We drew the first and then lost the next two of our opening three games. Around this time, the ownership of the club changed hands, with lifelong fan Jack Walker taking over. There was immediately talk of investment but we didn't see it right away. There was certainly no way of knowing the transformation of the club that was about to happen in a remarkably short time. There was a gymnasium for the team in a derelict terraced house across the road from Ewood Park and the manager's office was upstairs in the house. It was a throwback to the 1950s and 60s in many ways. Medical facilities were so threadbare you'd go to the hospital.

One of the first changes was Kenny Dalglish coming in as manager. He and his assistant Ray Harford changed training and made it a lot more active and different. Kenny and I had differing allegiances from our backgrounds but we got on all right – I always felt that he was approachable enough to talk to. My experience of working with him was limited due to what was about to happen in the near future but he obviously went on to do very well for Blackburn. I know people say that he spent money but he is well revered at the club for winning them the league and that's all that matters. Kenny didn't have the best of managerial careers afterwards with Newcastle and a disappointing return to Liverpool but there are many examples of great players who didn't quite make great managers. Sir Bobby Charlton at Preston was another example.

Likewise, there are a fair few examples of managers like Jose Mourinho who weren't great players but decided early on to study the game and it has benefitted them in their managerial career. It's not always an obvious, self-fulfilling path. As I say, people accuse Blackburn of buying success, but with Jack being such a passionate fan of the club and so passionate about their success, I think they did it in the right way, even if I was about to become something of a victim of it.

I suffered an ankle injury in training just before Christmas 1991 and it was very sore, so I went to see a specialist at a Blackburn hospital. After examination, all he did was give me a cortisone injection, but it didn't really help. I knew that it was more than just swelling. A couple of days later, I was feeling my foot in the bath and felt a piece of bone in my ankle as if it was floating about. I went to the physio and asked him to look – he said I'd broken it. I had to have an operation to have it fixed, and in the meantime, the club signed a replacement on loan. I went into the club as part of my rehabilitation and saw the new lad in my training gear. Were they trying to tell me something?! Was there really not another kit or number he could have worn? That really didn't sit right with me.

I went to Lilleshall for more rehabilitation but by the time I was fit the team had really turned around and was picking up results in a promotion push.

Frank Stapleton was in charge at Bradford and asked if I fancied going there on loan to help with me returning to match-fitness. I enjoyed my short time there and when the loan ended, it seemed there was no future for me at Blackburn as they had David May playing in my position. Bradford had been impressed with me and said that if I found myself without a club, then I was more than welcome to go back there and they'd give me a contract. That decision was made fairly quickly in May, and then I watched Blackburn achieve promotion in the play-offs into the new Premier League. The turnover of players in that team was prolific and clearly there was no place for me.

It was disappointing to leave after the spell I'd had. Nothing had really worked out at Blackburn, I'd never had a proper chance to establish myself and prove myself to the supporters in as much as I didn't get to show them what I was capable of. Okay, I was a little past my best, but I was still capable of better than what I showed on the pitch during my spell at Ewood Park. As disappointing as it was, I had to move on. The club obviously had and already I felt like it wasn't a success I'd had a part of, reminiscent of those latter days at United.

Looking at everything in those later days of my career in England, it's quite funny – I left United just before they became successful, and also left Ewood Park just before their promotion to the Premier League which was when the financial boom in football really came in. There was no way of knowing the longevity of each of these but I'm sure I'm not alone in the fact that I did not see the commercial expansion of the game coming. It really is crazy.

One of the most commonly-asked questions for players of my era, is whether we are jealous of the modern-day player. Personally I'm happy with where I am in life and the path I took, and people forget there are pitfalls that come with the kind of money and profile that players get today. You see so many fail to make it because the money goes to their head. I got paid for kicking a ball around for 20 years and I'm well aware there are people envious of that. I don't know any of the modern-day players and can't comment on their characters but speaking of my generation, we were all approachable and I felt we were a good bunch.

Change is inevitable, you have to deal with it. I say that, but people would always come up to me and say, 'You've never changed.' I was still the same person! I was fortunate in the sense I was never the superstar of the team. If we went out with Norman Whiteside or Bryan Robson they'd be the ones getting the attention. I feel honoured that I was able to play alongside those two and feel that they could easily walk in to the United team of 2014 and improve it. Could I? Yes, I'm confident that at my absolute best I would be one of the players from the 1980s team to get in.

I was past my best but far from finished and it wasn't time to be nostalgic. In 1992, the game may have been on the verge of a seminal change, but I was simply at that next stage of 'natural progression'.

18

Over The County Border

I SHOULD probably go back and explain the move to Bradford City in more detail. Frank had come to watch me play for Blackburn's reserves and obviously made an approach to Kenny, who asked if I fancied going on loan for a few weeks to improve my fitness. Bradford were in the Third Division but league football was more competitive than the reserves and with the location not being an issue I felt it was a good move. Ironically enough, with the move being made for convenience, my first game there was at Torquay United on 1 February 1992.

It was a move that helped me return to full fitness but the more time I was away from Blackburn the more I was missing out on the momentum they were building with their run for promotion. When it came to the end of the season and considering what I'd do, realising I wasn't likely to be in contention for a starting role at Ewood Park, I decided to stay on with Bradford.

Despite the injuries that I had started to pick up, and the fact that I was 32 going into 33, I hadn't given any consideration to finishing. Fitness had been a big part of my game but because the ankle injury had been an impact one rather than my body's way of telling me to give up, I hadn't really given retirement a moment's thought at that time. As a professional athlete it's not so much that you feel invincible as the belief that you just don't believe you'll suffer from these kind of injuries, or your recovery will be fairly comfortable and rapid. Time does catch up with us all and I was having to adapt my game. I was no longer able to match everybody in a foot race – I wasn't slow by any means but I could feel the changes.

In hindsight it looks like the wrong decision to move from Blackburn just as they were heading into the Premier League but just as I made the move there for the integrity of my career, I knew I had to move on for the same reasons. I'd felt out of place since the player came out for training wearing my number. And the destination once I knew I had to leave was again determined by the clubs in for me rather than my own preference. And in fairness, the fact that Bradford had already made it clear they wanted me was really encouraging. It's always nice to be wanted and it was a boost to my ego as a professional that everybody seemed to want me at Valley Parade. It compensated for the extra divisional drop, that's for sure.

You can move from Manchester United to anywhere and it's going to be a step down so moving from Blackburn to Bradford might have been a similar step although I think, oddly enough, the poor conditions at Blackburn had helped prepare me. Bradford had had the disaster and had attempted to rebuild but training and medical facilities were not the greatest. In a way, it wasn't so different to how things were at Blackburn and I certainly wasn't dreading returning to Bradford for the 1992/93 season.

In fact that summer was probably a lot better than the one where I'd left United because at least I had a club to go to, I knew that my future was secure, and there is a lot to be said for stability. It felt like the right move, too.

Frank Stapleton the manager compared to Frank Stapleton the player was an interesting thing to observe. He hadn't struck me as someone who would go on to be a manager although he was of the nature to think about the game. Certainly more than I did – I'd go out and play and that was about it. Frank was doing his coaching badges at Blackburn but it always struck me as odd because he wasn't strict but he wasn't exactly laid back. He wouldn't have a laugh and a joke with the players but at the same time wasn't unapproachable. I don't know – maybe he was a disciplinarian, but because I'd spent so long with him as a player, it was hard to see him in that way! We weren't socially friends at United (by that I mean that we never went around each other's houses for dinner or anything like that) although we never had any fallings out. It was just going to take a little bit of getting used to seeing him as the manager.

I suppose there may well be a tendency to expect someone who has played for Manchester United to attempt to play in a similar attacking fashion when they become a manager. It's not always so easy. I would think that in an ideal world all managers would love to play free-flowing attacking football but at Bradford we simply had to play to the strengths of the team.

Those strengths had only been good enough to finish in the middle of the Third Division in recent years but we were quietly optimistic at the start of the season and that translated itself into good results. By early November we were top of the league on goal difference but we then suffered a few injuries – our centre-halves were out, disrupting our defence, and our winter form saw us drop out of the play-off spots.

For whatever reason I didn't feel as if I personally was playing to the best of my ability, just the same as when I was at Blackburn. It hurt personally and professionally – every player accepts that you'll go through a dip in form, and the only way to get out of it is by working hard. I'd always resolved to do that in the past and even though I was playing in the third tier of English football I still had the desire to do so. I'm sure there may well have been players who had dropped down the divisions and were going through the motions at the back end of their careers but I still had that desire to achieve something. I had come out of a bad time before with what I felt was poor form for United in the 1980s but as genuine as the motivation is to do better, physically, it becomes harder to put things right. If you can't get it right, does that mean you're physically not capable anymore? I wasn't ready to accept that but there was only the odd game at Bradford where I showed what I was capable of. If I'm being overly-critical then maybe my own poor form was a part of the reason that our collective form tailed off.

The most memorable game in that first year at Bradford was not in the league but the FA Cup at Preston. It was on astroturf and wasn't the prettiest encounter – I ended up with a few stitches after a clash – but we won 5-4. Ultimately, it counted for nothing as we were eliminated in the next round. And although we should have at least got in the play-offs, we lost our last two games to miss out which was desperately disappointing considering we'd won four on the bounce to give ourselves a great chance.

I'd had a couple of problems with my knee – it sounds like a likely story but it gave way on the dance floor during a Christmas party. I'd had a few drinks but it still didn't feel right. Every now and again afterwards it would give out on me – I can remember one time during training in a public park, just going through drills, that I collapsed under it.

During our penultimate game at Leyton Orient it happened again so I went to the physio and ended up having my knee cleaned out over the summer.

There was a post-season break in Torremolinos where Frank and Stuart Pearson who had joined as assistant encouraged me to go out and join them. It was an opportunity to drown our sorrows. Disappointing as it was, it's much better to have come close than do nothing and it was a huge improvement for Bradford.

There had been a delay on our summer plans because of the potential play-off berth we were fighting for and I remember at the time there was still actually a lot of controversy over whether the play-off system was a good thing. I think over time it has proved to be so although you have to feel sympathy for the third-placed team if they miss out. How often have you seen a team sneak into sixth place, benefit from the momentum and get promotion?

In 2014 our lads at school got through to the cup final at Wembley where they were the northern representatives, playing on the day of the play-off final between QPR and Derby County. It's a great occasion for the clubs involved and I think has been a great addition to the football calendar even if I can understand the grumbles from those who miss out.

I was long gone from Old Trafford but was still missing out when the club won the league in 1993. I was happy to see their wins in the European Cup Winners' Cup and the 1992 League Cup but I have to admit there were mixed emotions in 1993. I dearly wished I'd been a part of it. I don't mind openly admitting to feeling envy towards them, particularly as they'd managed to be that group of players who had won the first league title after so long. United's subsequent lorry-load of trophies has been easier to take and no-one has been happier for them than I have but to be so close yet so far away. Clayton, Robbo, and Steve Bruce – I was happy for them, yet it bit at me that I wasn't part of it.

'So close yet so far' might as well be the subtitle of my book – it was like that with Blackburn, and like that in the summer of 1993 with Bradford City. On the verge of a great achievement, we'd stumbled at the last. There was a huge desire to go forward but my knee problem was more serious than I'd first thought and it had a damaging impact on my first-team chances.

I only managed to play 13 times in my second season at Bradford but even when I was on the pitch I was well below the standard I'd come to expect from myself. On one return to the first team against York on a cold Saturday in January, I was so poor that I was dropped to the reserves to play against Barnsley in the week. It was stop-start all the time and, in fact, to say it started at all would probably be an overstatement. It was similar for the club who never really managed to mount a serious promotion push. We finished in seventh, one place below the play-off places, but that was due to winning our last two games – after 44 games, we'd been in tenth, nine points off any chance of promotion through the back door.

One bright spot that year had been the emergence of Graeme Tomlinson. He scored a few goals and was noticed by Manchester United. Alex Ferguson and Brian Kidd were at a couple of games to watch him and I have to confess it was a bit of a surprise – he was a good talent, and probably deserved a chance at a higher level, but always appeared to me one of those players that could go either way. I wasn't surprised that a big club took the gamble on him but equally I wasn't shocked that it didn't really work out. I know injuries weren't kind to him but maybe all things considered it was the wrong move at the wrong time.

Graeme was one player highly regarded at the club, as were Dean Richards and Phil Babb. Dean was a tidy defender, as was Phil, but I didn't feel that either were outstanding. Dean of course developed at Wolves and then earned his move to Spurs – he had good times at both clubs. That's not to pull Dean down, I just didn't note his potential as being remarkable during our time together at Bradford, though admittedly I may have been spoiled from having grown up around the likes of Martin

Buchan and seeing players come through like Kevin Moran. Not that I was in a position to judge, being so disappointed with my own form as I was.

The raised levels of expectancy from the previous season meant that Frank was under pressure from the board and our sub-standard performance in the 1993/94 season meant that it was more or less inevitable that he would lose his job. There were no mass protests or any bad feeling towards Frank, no animosity – at least to my recollection – but things going the way they had meant that he wasn't going to remain at Valley Parade.

Neither was I. The chairman released a lot of older players and I was one of them, back on the PFA list of players available. Curiously enough, for the first time, I began to attract a lot of interest from abroad. Gordon Milne was manager of Besiktas but at the end of the season left his role so that interest never materialised any further; there was contact from a Portuguese Second Division club whose name escapes me now. Then out of the blue we got a call offering me a deal in Hong Kong. Having been there previously and enjoyed my time there I felt it was a good opportunity to detach myself from England and get something back – it seemed like a really great move that I'd be crazy to turn down, but also an opportunity for the family.

I had been as motivated as ever but there was no denying that two downwards moves in English football had taken its toll on my confidence so when the opportunity arose to do something which was so far removed from the domestic game that you are talking in terms of lifestyle rather than the relative standard of the game then it opened my eyes to the bigger picture.

You may be wondering if seeing Frank deal with the pressures of being a manager at such close quarters influenced my decision to not go into that side of the game. The truth is that I never had any interest in it. I had some interest in working with young players but I knew management was definitely not for me and I hadn't helped out with any coaching at any time at Bradford. I did start doing my Level 1 qualification in coaching while I was there with the Lancashire FA over at Burnley. I enjoyed it but I didn't have any thoughts about where it was leading – Level 1 is simply about basic drills, shooting and passing.

There wasn't an analytical side to it although those with a propensity to be analytical obviously take it that way. There were a mixture of people, professionals, teachers, and Joe Public. I went all the way to doing my UEFA B badge some years later when I was teaching, on the same course as Brian McClair and Kevin Bond. The PFA were doing the course at The Cliff, funnily enough, and because I'd had two or three years in teaching, I found a lot of what I was doing lent itself to coaching. I think I actually found it easier than doing Level 1 because of the time of life I was at, and the teaching had helped so much that it was untrue. The coaches running the course took me aside and encouraged me to do the A Level, but I just felt it wasn't right for me.

Having been offered the opportunity to carry on playing in Hong Kong back in 1994, I didn't even have to entertain the notion of doing anything other than concentrating on my own performance. Well, that and the small matter of, for the first time, leaving the north-west!

19

Fragrant Harbour

THE decision to move to Hong Kong was one I had to make but not one I felt a responsibility for, if that makes sense. I didn't have many options on the table after my contract was up at Bradford and as I've already said, the Hong Kong offer was so appealing for everything that was there aside from the football that I would have been mad to turn it down.

Experienced players at the end of their careers can sometimes move to developing leagues – we've seen in recent years that there have been many lucrative moves based on finance to places like Australia and North America. The lifestyle must be good there too, don't get me wrong, but the incentive is normally very clear. The Hong Kong league, by contrast, has been established for around a century and wasn't seeking to win any popularity contests. There was the case of the odd big name going out there – George Best played a couple of games in the country – but usually it was a case of professionals like myself trying to extend their careers for a couple more seasons. If anything, I think they were trying to boost the local popularity of the sport.

It would be logical to question the rationale of someone who turned down a move to Wolverhampton because it was too far from the north-west and just a few years later moving halfway around the world. I would never complain about the lifestyle that football had given me but if there had been a couple of drawbacks it had been that despite visiting some great places, I'd never got the opportunity to see the true beauty of them, and probably more importantly than that, my family hadn't been with me. The move gave a chance to finally eliminate that problem and perhaps most importantly of all, our boys were both at an age where they would benefit from the cultural experience and not have it harm their education. More than it being an opportunity for me, it was one for the entire family. It wasn't only the right time but perhaps the only time that chance would come up.

The whole of the family were excited by the change, Karen certainly was and the kids were of a good age. Ashley would have had two more years at primary school and we rationalised it as the opportunity to have two good years there and then move back to have him ready for senior school.

Football-wise, I was hopeful of some re-invigoration. The club I was joining was Golden, a newly-created club in the country. I went out with Gary Williams, who had played for Aston Villa and won the league and European Cup there, as he had been at Bradford with me. We weren't exactly superstars but we were being treated as players who had accomplished a lot and it was quite nice to arrive with a reputation that hadn't been damaged by my days since I'd left Old Trafford. It was something that I'd needed since I left United. Once you go from there you're never rid of the reputation – not that I wanted to be – but you have to try and live up to it. Sadly it didn't work out at Blackburn but once you go from Blackburn to Bradford and things don't work out then you're close to the footballing scrapheap and that was something I was wary of. In all senses it was the kind of boost I needed at that point in my life.

I was glad to have Gary as someone I knew to accompany me although we knew there was a strong English-speaking contingent already there like Lee Bullen, who went on to be a cult hero at Sheffield Wednesday, as well as Carlton Fairweather who had been at Wimbledon. Sadly Gary didn't settle in as well as we did so left after the first season. That happens sometimes, people get homesick or just can't adapt to the culture, but for whatever reason it was, it can't have been down to the hospitality, as we couldn't have been made more welcome.

We were actually asked to fly out on the day of the 1994 World Cup Final between Brazil and Italy in the USA. Gary and I refused because we didn't want to miss the game, so asked if we could go the day after. Unbeknown to us, a welcome reception had been set up for us in a hotel on that day. The first group of players who were going over still went out but as it turned out they moved the reception to accommodate us. It was a nice welcome as soon as we arrived and there was a press conference with assorted journalists which made it feel like a big deal.

Sadly the actual living accommodation wasn't the best to begin with. It was okay as it was only temporary – we had a month before the families flew out to join us so we had plenty of time to find a place. It was more trouble adapting to the heat, humidity and climate knowing it would be a permanent thing we'd have to deal with. It was strange – that was a place we'd flown to for pre-season, but our pre-season for Hong Kong involved flying to Vietnam! The owner, Simon Wan, had business out there and was mixing work with pleasure. We were promoting Golden out there and played a few games which was a hell of an experience in itself.

Vietnam is of course a culturally significant place in world history, particularly the 20th century with the war, and it was a totally different experience to anything I'd been through or witnessed before. Everything appeared to be at street level – people were working, cooking, out on the street. You'd see dads riding motorbikes with their kids on the handlebars. Again, though, we saw the footballer's insular, protected version of it. So I say it was an experience but probably more of a visual one. I'd have liked to have seen a bit more but was grateful for what I did.

In Hong Kong, however, I was able to have the experience I'd wanted to have when I'd been there before. There's a lot to the country that people don't know or aren't aware of. Around half of Hong Kong is land that is dedicated as country parks; people see the waterfront and the skyscrapers but behind that, there are the outlying islands you can visit. Initially when I got there I lived just outside the racecourse at Happy Valley where we would train on the pitches inside but we were looking for nice places with the greenery and the local lads couldn't believe we wanted to live 20 minutes away.

For them, you had to be on the doorstep to have shops and restaurants. You didn't need a car on the island, I didn't know why anyone would have one – everywhere was safe to work and the public transport system was tremendous. We had to think about our families so didn't want somewhere too busy and so we found a place to stay called Discovery Bay, on Lantau Island. The island itself is twice the size of Hong Kong island at 56 square miles but with a population of only 45,000 compared to Hong Kong's 1.4 million. There was a multicultural community where no cars were allowed – you'd get on to the main island by a ferry which took 30 minutes. It easily passed with a brew or a book and served as a good amount of time to come down after training.

Discovery Bay had everything you could need, lots of recreational opportunities, so was the perfect place. It felt like a dream, it was unbelievable. The club were paying for our accommodation which was helpful as the cost was so high. I felt like I had a new lease of life, and no longer was it an effort to get out of bed in the morning. Okay, the quality of the football wasn't as high but we had some good players and good games. Training was just as intense and we worked just as hard as anywhere I'd been before. We trained at 4.30pm so we had all day to partake in the leisure activities, swimming and so on. I'd be back by 7pm so had the rest of the evening free. It was almost like a big holiday for the kids although they did have to be taught – we got an English tutor to teach them in the afternoons. At the time, everyone spoke English, which I suppose doesn't really help you when you're emigrating. We did try and learn a few of the basics to get by to help to integrate into the wider community.

Because all of the teams played games at the same venue, Mong Kok Stadium, it meant that there wasn't a clearly defined calendar in the sense we wouldn't play every Saturday. Games were on a rotation. Special games would be played in Hong Kong Stadium, such as cup finals, and that depended on whether you could book it. After games we'd go for meals with the team. Around half of the lads were Chinese and then you would have some Eastern Europeans, smatterings of different nationals.

The Chinese lads would eat their traditional food but we were known as 'Gweilo' which I think was an old word for 'ghost'. We'd eat food that was tailored to European tastes. We didn't exclude ourselves purposefully, sometimes we'd request to eat the same food as them, and we learned to use chopsticks and everything. Gweilo is apparently meant in some circles as a derogatory term but we never took it like that. I think it was important for us to try and embrace as much of the culture as we could.

The style of football was very European, influenced by the quality of the players who came over. Golden had just entered the Hong Kong league but there were a lot of established teams in there like South China, who I'd played against before with United. South China had their own ground which was an athletics venue. Instant Dict were another, Rangers another. Every now and again you'd get a businessman starting a franchise and Golden was one of those – they'd been around a few years but we were the start of the rebirth, if you like. All of the players in that first pre-season were in the same boat, trying to get to know each other. There was Ian Hesford, and Dale Tempest (better known for betting in later years), who played for Eastern AA, and they were the team to beat. They were connected to one of the local newspapers.

We played well, especially for a newly built side, and even in the games we lost we managed to give a good account of ourselves. Eastern won the league the first time around and Instant Dict, another solid side, won it in our second year. In the second season, we qualified for the cup final, where we lost to South China 4-1. It was closer than the scoreline suggested, in fairness to ourselves.

I think some of the expats and even some of the locals were surprised by how we, as a group, pushed ourselves. I'd like to think that my professionalism was part of the reason I'd been brought over in the first place and I certainly wasn't there for a holiday. I was pushing myself as hard as anybody, and I'd be at the front running in training if I could. I had to adapt to the climate and though it was tough, I was able to do it. We had a warm spell in the UK in the summer of 2014 where people complained about humidity and it made me laugh because it was nothing compared to what we faced in Hong Kong. You could be sat having a conversation and be dripping with sweat – it wasn't anything to do with health, it was simply how it was. I was drinking water and taking on fluids at a rate that was alien to me, although, I have to say, it was different but not difficult. Having been exposed to the climate in previous years, albeit for shorter periods, I was aware of what I needed to do to remain healthy and sensible. Maybe it was because on pre-season trips, you're working vigorously to prepare, and here we were training in 'regular' seasons, it appeared easier. Maybe as a consequence, my injury problems had more or less cleared up completely.

Golden finished third in both seasons I was there; the second season was split into stages and we were just one win off finishing in top spot in the second stage, which would have put us into the Grand Final. We would have played South China, around the same time as the cup final, so third best was probably a true reflection of where we stood in comparison.

I think it would be completely generous and in all honestly probably misleading to say that in my time there, there was a significant advance in the quality of the game. The standard was what it had been; the most positive thing I'd like to think that I contributed was my attitude and hopefully that rubbed off in a positive way on others. The insular attitude to the promotion of the game perhaps goes some way to explaining the lack of advancement on the international stage. Hong Kong, like India, is one of the largest populations to not have an accordingly successful football output. In fairness, a lot of Hong Kong is Americanised, so to that end sporting interests were on the main ones they were exposed to seeing from North America and football/soccer was something enjoyed by the minority, even if that minority took it really seriously. Premier League football was enjoyed on television, but again, within that relative minority. Manchester United were still a big deal and I'd been to the area before so I was quite well known. Crowds for the games weren't massive – you'd normally be happy with 1,000.

That said, there was significant interest when it was announced the England national team would be coming over as part of their preparations for the Euro 96 tournament that was actually being held *in* England. When it was first revealed to us as something that was being considered by Golden we thought it was a massive step – we thought we were a decent enough side but there's that and then the level of playing internationally. When it was formally announced, there was no point feeling any trepidation, we had to prepare ourselves for the real business. 'Business' included seeking any possible advantage and a suggestion to play them at the hottest part of the day due to us being more comfortable in the climate. That was rejected, and as it transpired, it lashed it down anyway!

The build-up really was intense. There was a Japanese team touring at the time and we used the opportunity to play them at Mong Kok as a warm-up. They were a hell of a side. It was a great test, as they played fairly quick and it was a good pace for us to get used to as we expected England to play at a slower pace due to the conditions.

Dave Watson, the former Everton defender, had been invited to come over and represent us in the game, while Iain Hesford came and took part as our goalkeeper. There was talk of all kinds of players like Gabriel Batistuta coming to play for us but that never came to fruition.

It wasn't the best of tours for England – controversy seemed to be following them, and we sensed opportunity.

I was now 36 years old. Having initially figured to spend two years in Hong Kong and coming towards the end, I hadn't given too much thought to officially retiring, but by the same token, I hadn't really considered where I would move to next. I'd enjoyed playing football out there but for the first time our next move, which we intended to make back to England, was being made with the education of the boys as the main thing. It was only when it came around that the England game was seriously going to go ahead that the timing of it began to realistically represent what would probably be my last game of professional football. And what a way to go out. That said, it wasn't the foremost consideration in my mind that I'd be playing my last game. It was more like a cup final.

On the day, we more than held our own. I hadn't captained Golden in my time there but for this game I was given the armband. I felt a little selfish as one of the local lads, Lee Fuk Wing or 'Foxy' as we called him, was the regular skipper. David Platt was England captain and it was good to have a conversation with him as I hadn't seen him since he'd left United as a youngster. It finished 1-0 in a pretty even encounter with chances for both sides. Les Ferdinand scored early on but they weren't convincing – Lee Bullen had a one-on-one with David Seaman where he should have scored. We'd been promised a really good bonus if we scored, though we didn't hold it against him. I think he felt bad enough, particularly being a Scot! As captain, I was presented to meet Chris Patten, the Governor of Hong Kong, who spoke really nicely to us.

The evening before we'd gone up to Sha Tin Racecourse to have a meal with the England team. Bryan Robson was there as assistant to Terry Venables so it was nice to see him; in the party were the Neville brothers, who I'd never met before, but by this stage they'd broken into the Manchester United first team. I went and introduced myself to them, starting with, 'I don't know if you remember me,' and their response was so enthusiastic and humbling, calling me their hero. They'd just won the league and cup double! They were lovely lads. Gary had established himself as United's first-choice right-back although Phil had played some games there towards the end of the season and it was Phil who started in the position for England. I swapped shirts with him – he'd asked me at Sha

Tin and I was more than happy to do so. All of our other lads wanted Alan Shearer's shirt. We were given footballs to throw out to the crowd after the game – I spotted the boys and Karen so I just went over and handed mine to them.

It wasn't recognised as an official international match so the England players weren't capped and we didn't receive anything for it either. After all, technically, we were representing Golden in an 'XI' side, rather than Hong Kong. Coincidentally enough, there was an annual competition called the Carlsberg Cup held every February and I played in a Hong Kong representative side that faced Sweden as well as others. We were managed by Tony Sealy, the former QPR player. That was a side made up of the best players from all the teams in the league. By routine, everything was in the style of an international game, although it wasn't recognised as such because we weren't Hong Kong natives. I'd missed the first Carlsberg Cup through injury but was selected for the second.

After the England game we went out to an area of Hong Kong called Aberdeen to have a meal. Originally, it was an old fishing village, but it was now very built up, and it was – and still is – home to a very famous floating restaurant, Jumbo, which we had to get a ferry across to. Both sides were there and it was to be our last night in Hong Kong as we were flying back the day after.

There couldn't have been a better way to end. *The Independent* went as far as to say I (as well as Dave Watson) should get recalls to the national side on that showing but although it was a very nice thing to be said it was clearly intended as more of a criticism of the players of that period. At the time, we weren't aware of that kind of coverage, but looking back it was nice to see. I was just happy to have done myself justice. It's probably somewhat ironic that I was given more praise for playing against England than I ever did playing for my country! Dave and I must regularly feature in pub quizzes for that game. Iain had never won a senior cap but, funnily enough, was in the under-21 squad with me that won against Germany.

I say that it was a good way to end. That's with the benefit of hindsight, as at the time, I was still undecided. My thoughts of the future were focused on the immediate, such as returning home and getting the kids back into school. If I was distracted by any thoughts during the game at all it was more likely to be associated with packing suitcases than packing it in. It may well have been for the best that I wasn't consciously aware that it was my last game as it may have affected my performance.

Fresh out of contract, available just before pre-season and with a fairly decent showing of myself against England, you might have thought that arriving back in the UK, I would have had an offer waiting for me of some kind. That's not to say that I was expecting one, or even that I was disappointed when I didn't get one. I phoned around local clubs asking if I could go and train and ended up going to Accrington Stanley just to keep my fitness up just in case. I played a couple of minutes as a substitute in their pre-season but nothing came of it.

A few years back I'd been interviewed by a local paper who had asked me what I expected to be doing in the next five years. I'd said, tongue in cheek, 'Managing Accrington Stanley in the Football League.' Whether that had been noted by the manager at the time, and he had felt threatened either in the short term or long term, I wasn't contacted or kept on there. By that time I well and truly had no intentions of going into management as I wasn't management material. It just seemed to fade away and that was that for my football career. The way things transpired over a short period of time meant that my retirement, though never officially announced, came around fairly quickly. Over and done with no fuss whatsoever and the next chapter of my life – and this book – came around with a swift transition.

Some might say that the way my career ended summed up my entire journey – unassuming and away from the spotlight. It wasn't intentional. Nowadays players seem to be so full of self-importance that their retirement from club football needs to be announced (and sometimes international football, even when it's clear they won't be selected again – talk about stating the obvious) but because of the direction my life was moving in, I didn't feel it was relevant to put out any kind of announcement. Even to the family. I never even said to Karen, 'That's it.'

I did have one offer – Simon Wan had tried to keep me in Hong Kong and wanted me to go back. After the England game I'd told him we were returning to the UK and our reasons for it. I thanked him for everything and he was gracious enough about it although at the Jumbo restaurant that night he was even trying to convince the kids! They started crying, wanting to stay – Simon, you swine, I thought! Karen would have stayed too, I'm sure, but we had to think rationally and logically. We could have stayed another year, and who knows where it would have ended up. However, we'd made the decision to bring the kids back to put them in school – I just wasn't expecting that that's where I'd end up, too.

20

'In order to write about life – first you must live it.'

Ernest Hemingway

I PLAYED football as a professional for 20 years. Around the same amount of time has passed since my last professional game in 1996. When I think about it like that, it's strange that the opening chapter of this book talks about the first 15 or 16 years, this, the 20th, looks at the last 20, and the other 18 cover almost a year each. And yet I don't believe my life is governed, or defined, by football. Life since leaving the profession has been very fulfilling.

I wasn't one of those professionals who found it hard to leave the game behind. As soon as I landed back in the UK I started looking for work, as being out of work, we were dipping into our savings right away. I put together a CV and sent it around a few clubs with the hope of perhaps going into youth coaching rather than playing on. I went down to the Job Centre and looked in local papers for any opportunity. I wasn't too proud to do that – I had a wife and family to support and I wasn't going to ask for a handout. The boom of Sky TV was beginning to take hold so a lot of former players were becoming pundits.

I don't think I'm bubbly enough for that kind of thing, although I did cover a couple of games later on for Radio Lancashire. I don't think I ever came across as loudmouthed as a player so I wasn't an obvious choice to step into that kind of thing.

Those early days after returning to the UK were busy, with me looking for work and also the family settling into a new house. We had bought one before we went out to Hong Kong, an old farmhouse, and my old friend Tony Riley was overseeing the renovation and redecoration of it while we were away. This was in the days before e-mails so all our communication was done via fax and telephone. It was a bit like that scene in the movie *Lost In Translation* where Bill Murray's character is having to choose carpet samples! We basically had an entire kitchen fitted via fax.

Knowing we were coming back to a new house was something to look forward to, and I did. The house had a bit of land and I'd wanted to have some livestock and a few dogs, that was a bit of a dream of mine, so I was quite excited. Karen, on the other hand, took a long time to get used to being back in the UK. It didn't help that the house was a bit isolated. It wasn't easy to walk anywhere, you'd have to drive. Maybe if we could have moved the house into a better position Karen might have found it easier. To be fair, though, she never made a fuss about it at the time. It was only when we moved from that house that she revealed she was glad to be moving. I was in my element, revelling in getting some sheepdogs and walking around the countryside.

It was through the Job Centre that I actually managed to get my first job after football. I mentioned it right at the start of the book – I started working on the milk cart for Jackson's Farm, a local farm I knew well. They were one of the last in the area to deliver by horse and cart. It was something I could do, needed no qualifications, and I needed the money. There I was, getting up at 5am and driving an electric milk float. I had a week's training and then was allowed out on my own to deliver milk around the Accrington area.

I started doing a bit of part-time coaching at Blackburn, once in the week and once on a Sunday morning. Alan Irvine – who would go on to manage Preston, Sheffield Wednesday and West Brom – was the academy director there and he was contacted out of the blue by Chris Rigby, who had played with me at town team level. Chris said that Paul Mariner, the ex-Arsenal player, was coaching at Bolton School but had been offered a position in North America and so was leaving. There was, subsequently, a vacant position for the role of football coach. Alan was asked but said he had too much on – he suggested me for the position instead. I rang Chris up and he invited me for a chat where I was able to see the incredible facilities they had. The sporting facilities were as good as I'd seen at many Premier League teams at the time. The opportunity for a full-time role was too good to turn down – and after an interview with the headmaster, I was offered the job.

I had to give a week's notice on the farm, so for that first week at school I was doing the milk round in the morning and then drove to Bolton School to prepare to start at 10.30am. Jackson's had been great because they were trying to offer me extra work but they were able to understand that the security of a permanent full-time position wasn't something I could turn down. It had been the first time I'd really given serious thought to what I'd do for a career after football. I'd had my short spell at Accrington and would have been happy to play part-time but for whatever reason they didn't want to know; the Blackburn part-time job was nice but was never going to develop into something serious.

Starting at Bolton School was more or less my retirement call from playing football. There'd been something of a generational shift in the game. From leaving United to my spell in Hong Kong, I'd been out of the 'limelight', so to speak, for around six years, so the kids I was teaching, although they were of secondary school age, were just about too young to remember me at my peak. That was something that probably helped me settle. I didn't have any expectations from the kids, I just came in as a new teacher who was teaching them football. After a while, one or two of them did mention that their dad or granddad had said they knew who I was, or told me, 'Sir, I bought you on Championship Manager,' but it was only the odd comment. I was seen as a teacher and not a former footballer and I really do think that helped me settle in. In those early days I probably had as much to learn as the kids I was teaching. Staffroom etiquette and in the classroom, for example. I was able to find there were a lot of crossovers with teaching and coaching – the way you address people, the way you control your own discipline in order to maintain order.

Still, my background might have been unknown to some but it wasn't to me. I hadn't come through the same conventional system that other teachers had and so I felt like a bit of a fraud. I went to see the head, a gentleman called Alan Wright, who reassured me. He said I could kill myself for three years getting the qualifications or remain there, an independent school, and he would continue to employ me as a sports coach. He said I would be sent for qualifications in swimming, cricket and basketball for example. He was good to his word and I was able to enjoy the diversity that came with it. It was time for me to move away from solely concentrating on football. I'm not brilliant at all sports, but I try and put across that many of the same principles apply across the board aside from the particular techniques required for a sport. I've always said that my kids will never get a problem so long as they try their best. And, for eight years, I had an utterly rewarding time.

By that time in 2004, I had got the bug to want to go back abroad. I just wanted a change of scenery and location. After my coaching at Blackburn I'd been invited to go along to Manchester United's development centres to work with ten- and 11-year-olds. I'd go to The Cliff on Sunday mornings to oversee sessions around the time that Rene Meulensteen came to the club. Eventually, United agreed a huge sponsorship deal with Nike, and subsequently, the Soccer Schools programme was set up which had a loose connection with United. I was approached to see if I fancied a move back out to Hong Kong as head coach so I discussed it with the family. I wasn't surprised that Karen was instantly enthusiastic and so was Ryan. Ashley, on the other hand, wasn't keen – he was courting a girl and had a good job at the local sports centre. Ryan was working there too but was happy to leave his job. Ashley was 20 so we had a bit of a tough decision to make.

We had moved house again, to a residence that was always intended to be temporary. We had picked a house but the person didn't want to move! So we were due to move out of our house on the Tuesday but didn't have a new place by the time we'd got to the weekend before. We couldn't let the sale go because it was a good price; somebody told us at the last minute about a place that was available to rent, so we went there for six months until finding another house that was also going to be temporary, though we bought it this time. Ashley had settled in there and after much discussion we decided to make the move and leave him behind. It wasn't an easy thing to do.

There was some excitement with the opportunity but a lot of unknown paths we were walking down. Things like setting up direct debits for Ashley so he didn't have to worry about the bills, the fact that we weren't entirely sure just what was going to go on with the Soccer Schools. I had a two-year contract there but we weren't quite sure what the set-up was. And Karen, having originally been so enthusiastic, was now torn. It took her a long while to settle back into life in Hong Kong and she couldn't bring herself to speak to Ashley on the phone for quite some time as it made her so upset. He did come out – he actually spent his 21st birthday with us and a lot of players I'd played with in the mid-1990s came to a big party. Ryan came along as a coach – he was doing his badges anyway and it had become a condition of me moving over there that Ryan was on the staff.

Before moving back to Hong Kong, being involved with the Soccer Schools at United had seen us go on a number of long-distance trips. There was one to North America, and one in Hong Kong too for the Nike Cup, and I think it was that trip in particular which really whetted my appetite to go abroad again. I would casually look for situations abroad anyway so when the Soccer Schools came up with the programme it seemed perfect.

It was nice to be associated with the club again, however loosely, as technically we were employed by Nike and the Soccer Schools name was essentially a wing of United's wider community efforts. Nike's commitment was something like a 13-year investment. For such an approach I don't think Nike's vision was the clearest, and it led to some confusion for the kids who came along. It was perhaps natural to think that being on the programme, they would enhance their opportunity to be spotted by United and possibly get a trial or even a contract. Some really talented players came on that belief. Others came just for enjoyment. As coaches, we weren't allowed to push or influence even if we saw real promise. I think a few of us were as misled or disillusioned as the kids at the end of it.

Don't get me wrong, there was a structure and a clear programme – better players would go into a development programme after being in our school, but it was the step after that which wasn't too clear. I also think that somewhere, somebody had been a little naive with their marketing. 'Build

250

it and they will come', relying on the name alone. Hong Kong, however, already had many, many activities for those same kids. It was left to other people to decide and arrange, people on the business side, but they seemed more interested in the appearance and things like the website. Sometimes we didn't even have footballs or proper accommodation. Appearance is important but is it more important than two of our coaches arriving in Hong Kong without a place to live, as happened at the start of our second year? I would probably have appreciated being consulted for my advice. I had enough experience.

After two years in Hong Kong, things seemed to be going stale to say the least. There was another school being run in Dubai and when the management came to see us at the end of the two-year spell, I suggested a switchover for some of the staff in the schools as it might not only freshen up the staff, but it might help the children also. I was interested, for certain, and the bosses agreed so we made that change.

Dubai was featureless compared to Hong Kong but I loved it all the same. A safe place to live and good facilities to work with. Their working week was a little different. They finished their weekly work at Thursday lunchtime so their weekend sessions would be Thursday evening and Friday morning. We enjoyed the change but towards the end of that first year, we learned that Karen's mother was getting ill. Naturally, Karen felt a pang to return. We hadn't stayed out there all year round – we'd return to the UK when the seasons were through and I would work at Old Trafford in the offices for six months because I was contracted for the year. I did one or two corporate things which were okay but I didn't enjoy the office. The second year, I told them that if I didn't have anything meaningful to work on, they could just pay me for the six months and not pay for the rest.

We went back out to Dubai for that third year and came back to the UK for Christmas – landing on the day of Ryan's

21st, which saw us celebrate accordingly. But those last few weeks after we returned east were very difficult for Karen with her mum being diagnosed with Alzheimer's. For anybody who has come across dementia in the family it really is hard to take. From being an active and involved mother of five, Vera was dependent on others. As the archetypal matriarch it was a real source of frustration for her that she couldn't do things she was used to such as cooking and cleaning, just everyday chores that she once took for granted. Added to this, Karen's dad had to have a heart-connected operation in the summer of 2008. It wasn't a major bypass but something that was needed at the time. The operation went well but the aftercare left a lot to be desired. He was sent home to fend for himself, given a few packages of padding for any leakages, but it wasn't sufficient.

Sadly, this culminated in his death on 22 December. As you can imagine, we were all devastated and apart from immediate funeral arrangements we also had to think about placing Vera in care. While speaking to Vera and mentioning Brian's death, she didn't seem to be taking anything in, and even at the funeral she was quite confused. Ultimately she must have realised because sadly, less than two months later, through missing her soulmate, she died of what was surely a broken heart. This illness is now affecting my own father with him suffering from vascular dementia. He seems quite different to Vera, in that he's happy go lucky, and if I can compare it to anything, it's really like going back to childhood.

Moving back in time a little and one day, towards the end of our stay in Dubai, we went out to Abu Dhabi, and I got a phonecall from Ashley. He told me Ferney had just rung – Paul Fernside, someone I'd worked with at the senior school – and wanted me to call him. I did, and Paul told me that a job had just come up at the primary school. The lad working there had gone up to the senior school.

My body started tingling – it was incredible. Without hesitation I asked Paul what I should do, so I immediately called the headmaster and sent in an application form to go through the formalities. That was in 2006 and I've been back at Bolton School ever since.

There are differences teaching kids of a younger age. Some learning can be 'drip, drip', but it's very rewarding. The head had asked me why I left teaching. The reality was I never had. I hadn't wanted to leave teaching, I just needed a change of scenery. If I could have taught abroad, I would have done. But I had no doubt whatsoever that it was right to go back. It felt so right.

As for the future, who knows? Karen always said, 'This is the last time!' whenever we've moved somewhere but something's always cropped up. I consider myself so lucky to have had two careers that have given me so much. In May 2014 the school football team got to Wembley for the Schools Championship. It was my seventh 'club' appearance there (my first at the new Wembley) and I was proud as anything to see the boys win.

I'm very proud of my sons, too – they both married in 2014 and do jobs they're very good at. As long as they are happy, that's all that matters to me. In sports, Ryan was probably more naturally gifted, but Ashley would compensate with his hard work. Both of them are talented swimmers, ten times better than me, which they love to remind me of! They've found their own way – they're good cricketers too. I actually played with them for the third XI at our local club alongside Ferney as wicketkeeper. There was a good mixture of good players and a few oldies. Ashley was the captain, and we won the league! That was a special moment for us all.

As fortunate as I consider myself to have the wonderful careers I've had, never a moment passes when I don't appreciate the sacrifices Karen has made for me throughout our life together. I think it shows in how I've written my story, or at least, I hope it does. She'd laugh at the suggestion that she's a career woman but she has still done a lot of things to support me and made a lot of tough decisions along the way and it means so much to me.

Hopefully she's done with having to make sacrifices now because I know just how good it feels when letting go of them. As crazy as it seems, my first Christmas in teaching in 1996, I was able to sit down to a Christmas dinner and eat it and have a glass of wine. Or a few! I can remember that first one so vividly. The concept of eating and drinking what I wanted was almost alien. That was the trade-off, I suppose. Even when I was playing, people would say, 'Well you get six weeks off in the summer, that's your Christmas,' but it's not the same. In Hong Kong I think we even played on one Christmas Day. We still got up with the kids in the morning and Karen did a great job at making it special with makeshift trimmings, paper chains that you don't tend to see these days. But it was presents and then football.

Having got myself in such a routine over the years, what I find most exhilarating at weekends now is the opportunity to do whatever I want. Even, simply, nothing. The everyman weekend. A reflection of who I am, perhaps.

Reflecting isn't something that always comes easy to me. I've got through this okay, though. People always tend to want to know or ask your best this, that or the other. It would be near on impossible for me to name a best XI from players I've played with for fear of leaving someone out but one thing that I'm not afraid of saying is that I'm confident that a number of players I played with could walk into and grace any Manchester United team.

There are obvious games and moments that stand out; my debut, cup finals, Barcelona, getting my first cap. But a 20-year career with 14 of those at Manchester United? That's crazy. It really is. To speak to the likes of Sir Matt, Jimmy Murphy, Sir Bobby and George Best. To be mentioned alongside the likes of Robson and Whiteside, to still be able to speak to them. It feels surreal sometimes. Just to be a part of it is something that I feel very fortunate about. To be a part of it is all I ever wanted. Everything and more I could have dreamed of. I'm not sure I appreciated it enough at the time, because I was in it. I certainly do looking back.

I am able to get just as much of a buzz or fulfilment from what I do now. At Bolton School Juniors there are lots and lots of events going on. We have a Christmas concert, and the kids performing really makes the neck hairs stand up. It's a million miles away from an FA Cup Final but gives me the same kind of feeling. I see it every year and I feel the same way. The innocence of youth really eradicates the cynicism of adulthood. At the end of every year, the Year Six pupils put on a school play which gives me a tremendous feeling.

That's what I'll take and remember. But how will I be remembered? 'A good solid professional', I expect, or words to that effect, in both of my chosen career paths. That's what people have said about me. I'm happy with that – it's great, and nice – but I'd like to think that maybe, without blowing my own trumpet, I was just a little bit more.